MOTH TALES

ANTHOLOGY

VOL. 2

APS Books
Yorkshire

APS Books
The Stables,
Field Lane,
Aberford
West Yorkshire,
LE25 3AE
www.andrewsparke.com

APS Books is a subsidiary of the APS Publications imprint

©2024 Phil Thomson
Cover design by Matt Johnson

The named authors have asserted the right to be identified as the authors of this work in accordance with the Copyright Designs and Patents Act 1988

All rights reserved.

First published worldwide by APS Books in 2024

No part of this publication may be reproduced, stored in or introduced into a retrieval system, or transmitted, in any form, or by any means (electronic, mechanical, photocopying, recording or otherwise) without the written permission of the publisher except that brief selections may be quoted or copied without permission, provided that full credit is given.

A catalogue record for this book is available from the British Library

FOREWORD

Writing has laws of perspective, of light and shade just as painting does, or music. If you are born knowing them, fine. If not, learn them. Then rearrange the rules to suit yourself.
Truman Capote

For some first-time readers, being in front of a microphone with what they have written is an ordeal they are willing to endure - discovering what their nerves are doing and how to control them, their folded papers shaking in their hand, head slightly bowed, voice measured. Then there are the assured performers, holding their mobile phones or their book at arms length - and occasionally, there are some who extemporise from an unfailing memory. All ages, so many differing backgrounds and one common purpose - each month they share their craft and creative journey with a listening audience in the convivial surroundings of The Moth & The Moon on Killigrew Street, Falmouth. Everyone is equal in front of the microphone. That is the spirit of Moth Tales.

Storytelling, rock and blues vibes, theatre, jazz, the ever present echoes of folk all have their roots in oral traditions and performance. What you will read here is a celebration of the spoken word, the anthology providing an opportunity for the word to go much further, whether read quietly in your own space, or performed just because it deserves to be heard. This book also gives writers the opportunity to look forward as the 'Moth' community expands. Poets, authors, dramatists are meeting other writers, going public, finding themselves published, sought after, appreciated and demonstrably, feeling good about themselves. And there's much more to follow.

Welcome to Moth Tales!

Phil Thomson

CONTENTS

SEBASTIAN ADAMS

Crust *1*
The protagonist's warming *2*
Procrastination of the web kind *3*
Altered alliteration *4*
45° *5*
The Empath Litany *6*

RHYS APOLLO

Shadows on the floor *7*
What. I think. You need to know *8*

ARCHIE

Herbal Skipping *9*
Words *10*
My break from work *11*
Time is taking its toll *12*

FRANCES BENNETT

Daffodils *13*
On Missing "The Legend of King Arthur" *14*
You are never far away *15*
Patchwork *17*

ALEX BLABY

Emerald Path - The Boy *18*
The long tomorrow - 'Bed' *21*

ZAK BOWDEN

Another day, another bolognese, *24*

LESLEY CHANDLER

Polly's Pancake Pantoum *25*

INDIA CHILDS

Two old men on a train from London to…? *26*

JAMES CROFTSON

Richer in the morning *33*
Simple pleasures *35*

KIM CROFTSON

I do not dress to impress *36*
Bus stop *37*
Wildlight *40*

ALAN CUMMINGS

The band has split up *41*
Daddies dancing *43*
Love lost in fourteen lines *44*
The epitaph *45*

MIKE DEMPSEY

No worries Dad *48*
Halo *50*

MAC DUNLOP

Untitled (excerpt) *55*
Time To Go *57*

CHLOÉ EATHORNE

Midnight Bike Rides with You *58*

LAUREN GAUGE

Poison Ivy *59*

VINCE GOULD

Let there be art *61*
In real time *63*

PAUL HACKETT

Gone but not forgotten *64*
I want to be a pirate *66*

DARSHAN HARODE

Home *67*

MAISY INSTON

My Marl *68*

JEREMY JOHNSON

The Black Book *69*
Too Basey *71*

PETER KING

Iron Tide Japan 2011 *72*

SIDDHARTH KUMAR

The wasteland is enchanted *74*

PETER MAXTED

Four by four *77*
Little England *79*
Kayakoy *80*

MATT MCCOY

The shopping trip *81*

SEBASTIAN RAMDIN

Busy Looking In Canterbury Kent *86*

ANDREW SEARLE

Lamb *87*
Every story that's ever been told *88*
Celestial Equator *89*
These Dancing Girls *90*

ALEX SMALL

Ageless Man *92*
Finger Tip *93*

PHIL THOMSON

Battery Road *94*
Living quarters, Causeway Bay HK *95*
Dunning Station *97*
Robbins of Dudley Punch Dagger *99*

FRANKIE DE VOS

A simple question *101*
The Parasite *102*
Stained glass storyteller *103*
Constellations *104*
Point Nemo *105*

GRENVILLE WATTS

Moon kiss *106*
Language *107*

CLARA ZOELLNER

The Artist *108*
Hectare of my heart *111*
Unsere Momente *115*
Green concrete *117*
Tainted *119*

Davaar
Heavens Might

MOTH TALES

SEBASTIAN ADAMS
Crust

A single empty pint glass this side of the bar,
the calling card of the not-my-job mentality.

Lined sedimentally with sentimental pauses,
each clear layer a gulp to forget.

Crusty foam leaves evidence of his thoughts,
the thicker ones harder to swallow.

White stained glass contrasts a chalk board,
Its user left with a less troubled mind.

What took you away an inch before the end?

I'll take it back for you, no worries my friend.

A gentleman stands this side of the bar
with a this-is-*my*-local mentality

Speaks loudly at staff with pronounced pauses
each deafly silence a point not to forget.

His speech leaves them evidently distraught
The thick noise makes it hard to hear

His paint-stained arm silhouettes against the light
directing troubles towards a table.

I've had enough of this pint an inch before the end

I'll just leave it here, no worries…

SEBASTIAN ADAMS
The protagonist's warming

The low white noise of distant motorways,
a baseline for robins to sing their morning welcome.

A sharp gentle breeze wakes my sleepy senses,
whispering preparation for the day ahead.

I stand by, watching windows viewing across the field,
Lego brick houses flash morse code from room to room,
writing biographical introductions to encrypted stories.

En mass, black confetti sprinkles the dawn-lit sky
Black birds dance their seemingly unorganised ritual,
unaware of their beautiful interruption

With their inward chatter now the soundtrack
of my patient solitude,
I wait with anticipation for light to break
between brick and nature,

The signal for where my story begins.

SEBASTIAN ADAMS
Procrastination of the web kind

With muffled conversations and distant dog greetings,
an unorganised flock of crows head west to roost.

Only a moment has passed since the rays touched the boundaries of green,
its source keen to carry the day elsewhere.

A moment of pause in a mountain of errands, as a spider continues with his.
The dim glow of the street illuminates its unfinished work,
my gaze captured by its crafted beauty.

As another silk thread is perfectly spaced, it reaches for the next join,
unaware that home for the night ahead
already had a victim of a different kind.

SEBASTIAN ADAMS
Altered alliteration

I love lust

A powerful primal statement,
two four-letter words with a reference to me,
their definitions desperately battling for control.

Ordinarily ordered, this way love has lost,
the referees retention only sees the immediate end,
the intensity primed for certain climax.

This electric elevation to the top
leaves no fulfilling foundation in wake,

And without a stable structure, the win will not hold.
A sudden slip of the wrist and lust becomes lost.

Its replacement of 'u' loses longevity,
solidifying its definitive demise.

I lust love.

A powerful context change,
Simply shuffling two strong words with a reference to me,
a statement controlled with defined definition,
an ordered battle; in a satisfying stalemate, nothing has lost.

No need for referees with no visible end in sight.

If the affection is carefully constructed,
its elevation evolves as I rise.
A joyful journey will leave me fulfilled.
I must keep this structure steady,
for I will want this infinitely.

But a slight slip of the wrist and lust becomes lost.
The replacement of you means I lost love,
my fearful fate.

SEBASTIAN ADAMS
45°

Does god only speak to me when I'm horizontal?
When my head hits the pillow, my thoughts become rational.

Things I should do, the things I should say and see.
The planning of my life,
The path I should take,
The ideas I have.

If I had enough paper and a pen with enough ink
I'd write down these thoughts as they spew out of my mind.
But I wouldn't have time or understanding to do most…..

I've always been told I'm laid back.
Maybe this is why my best ideas come when I am.

The light is off, the pillow is soft and I'm just drifting off.
An idea has popped up and now I'm thinking…

Should I risk it?

I'll remember it in the morning….. but I never do.
Reach for the light, find a pen…. (that I said I'd leave
by my bed for such an occasion)

Pen hits the paper, got one line written,
Wait! Got another
So I write that down.

One line,
Two line,
Three, four.

Quick refresh. What was the first one about again?
My head knows no boundaries when horizontal,
finds too many when vertical

That's it.

I'm going to start living
                        at a forty five degree angle.

SEBASTIAN ADAMS
The Empath Litany

The officiant says: I'm pretty much out there when it comes to my heart.

The people say: It's good and we like it, but can you bring it back in.

The officiant says: I capture what I can on paper to share what it can do.

The people say: It's good and we like it, but can you bring it back in.

The officiant says: Some say it's a weakness, if it is, why is it so hard?

The people say: It's good and we like it, but can you bring it back in.

The officiant says: I often think you can't hear me or that you're not listening.

The people say: It's good and we like it but can you bring it back in.

The officiant says: I don't know why I bother, I'm back at the start.

The people say: It's good and we like it but can you bring it back in.

The officiant says: This is not what I want and it's painful to do.

The Officiant & People say: It's good and we like it and we've brought it back in

RHYS APOLLO
Shadows on the Floor

All my fears are nothing more
Than shadows cast upon the floor
Terrifying abominable appearance
Lacking in logical coherence

Frightening figures flickering
Internal voices bickering
Defining the life that I live
Encasing me, restrictive

Brief lightning flashes momentarily dispel
Until egoic urges return and swell
A light must kindle deep within
Luminous love will always win

Shadows scream and beg to stay
Upon our heartstrings like harps they play
But don't be fooled by what is nothing more
Than shadows cast upon the floor

RHYS APOLLO
What? I think. You need to know.

Here's my funky biography
        I made it rhyme so it's fun to read
Born up North I fled down South
        To grow and heal by flapping my mouth
I had a wonky start to life
        Lots of misery, pain and strife
I capture it now upon the page
        Furiously scribbling out my rage
I sing of my past shameful antics
        And explore my mind's tocks and ticks
I'll ramble on about any subject
        Picking a topic to dissect and inspect
God, grief, tinder, cheese
        I write to heal,
           I
              write
                  to
                      please

ARCHIE
Herbal Skipping

No one told me there were so many hours in the day, that every minute was 60 seconds long and every second was 10 thoughts wide. That in it all there's every reason to be and to hate being. That this period of time is as long as you make it and that it all counts down again. I miss the skip button, the smokeable time machine, I miss not being up here all the time and knowing that I'm truly free to waste it all, I miss feeling satisfied by that knowledge and not scared of it. I miss waiting for time to speed up, not desperately fearing for the future, dreading the unspent minutes lingering in apathy, where information could pass through my brain like a revolving door with just enough to keep me entertained. Now, actively living is far more exhausting, making decisions is an everyday thing, an every moment thing, a constant pull asking myself what do I want, rather than a chase of happiness, No one told me it would be this relentless. No one told me it would be so easy to slip. I need stimulation and I need to go for a walk, because these four walls smell an awful lot like relapse and that a herbal blanket would truly stop my heart from racing. It's only 2:30 now. That feels like nothing till the day is done, but I have to do my best not to spend my days staring at clocks.

ARCHIE
Words

    Stuck in a rut for what, a small big thing that I rarely bring myself to live through, words looking at eyes, thoughts being transcribed into letters that try and form a unique sentence. It's been broken down too much maybe, the sounds and such, the words and that, they all are just things that we mutually agree on and exist and abide by and that means it doesn't exist.

    But the feelings do. The intention will usually shine through, the ways the words were written in surely they have a clue, the subject of the intention without exception surely surpasses and hopefully leads to catharsis, for feelings big and small, things wide and painfully tall, the rambling continues through the brain to the page, words tumbling out afraid of the stage at which they dissipate like cotton candy in water, lost ideas gone to the ethereal slaughter, only made real but physical active intention, between the thought and made their must be some tension. The hatred of the unstated things, a forgotten piece of art or a drawing that you always intend to start. It's muscle memory being creative that's why it's so incredibly debated; skill and talent play a role, but it's the lack of repetition that makes the soul turn cold. Where am going with this, thoughts circling like smoke caught between wind currents?

ARCHIE
My break from work

Soaking up the sun, photosynthesis, my eyes on the blue, I'm getting those rays, the wind in my hair, I'm getting some air, before the death of this freshness. Truth be told, this heat is discreetly frustrating, as I know these minutes will be some of the last with my skin absorbing the light for today, maybe tomorrow and maybe the day after. So angrily I'll sunburn, angrily I'll posture its vitamin importance before the long wait of work. On my break, I'll see u again but until then adieu to the great blue and that infrared collection.   It shall be sunny regardless of my exemption.

ARCHIE
Time is taking its toll

Time has taken a new meaning, a new method. Minutes do not count the same as before. They used to represent a length of boredom, and now they seem so small, so small.

Weeks pass in sentences, days pass in words, sometimes it will be hours before my thoughts are heard, sometimes they're all consuming, taking up my time. That's the problem with over-thinking and trying to make it rhyme.

Oh where oh where did all the days pass? Autumn was yesterday, I swear the leaves still held fast, and last week I can still remember, the summer breeze in the air, the days of bliss kissed my face with the sun bright and fair. I don't remember spring that was lost to time, but last winter was also a blur lost amongst the wine.

The days are lost to logic, a workload overthrown, a method to this madness shakes our sprightly bones, structure to the stress, distress amongst mess, methods and form betray our norms, oh the ways our brain does go.

FRANCES BENNETT
Daffodils

Deepest darkest secrets, we all have them
Some spill onto the street on a bright cold February day
Some are cheerfully confided on the number 47 bus
Some slip out as the future is faced with friends
But the angel trumpets of heaven still grow
In fields close by and on islands only an ocean away
And the bunches of bright yellow cut flowers spread out
Inviting conversation and lightening those secrets just for today.

FRANCES BENNETT
On Missing "The Legend of King Arthur"

I thought you'd come and see me, like so many others have done
And there's only one chance now
But I understand what happened that day;
Some of your party came, and whose carriage they came in
Was decided in advance, and no-one included you.
So then it would have been tomorrow
But you are indisposed.

I can see dust caught in autumn's sunshine
I gaze on those rays at distance,
My boat with its flowers stays put,
I'm not allowed to get any closer.
Like you, I don't always know what's going on
And I am so sorry we never met.
It would have been a love story;
Eyes across the gallery floor,
My everlastingly pre-Raphaelite pose
And you with your long hair
That people used to say was like mine.

I'm going away tomorrow
With all the other paintings
But keep the faith my dear
And one day we will
Gaze the one upon the other
One day in a distant city
Where I will hear the rumble
Of the traffic outside
And I will know that this time
You are on your way.

FRANCES BENNETT
you are never far away

i am surprised by street poems romantic inspirational and political
written on pieces of cardboard attached to trees tied with grass
adorning scaffolding all along the wire fence, punctuating
the monumental bulk of the old barracks in this city of golden stone

and now suddenly i am attending a free sunday morning poetry reading
ambushed again by this unexpected festival and this unseasonal
heatwave
a woman in bright clothes is saying, i'm not sure how long i've got
well I have several so I can choose
she and her friends stand right by my seat
in a buzz of Spanish pre-poetry reading event chatter

as if i have been given a prompt in writing class,
i look for pen and paper but all i have is my phone so
i start writing in this icloud notes page for the first time, going slowly,
revising, neglecting capitals, like i am turning into e e cummings
i am writing now; i might have one, choice is not an option,
but i could read this if i didn't plan to sneak out halfway through

today poems words and books, wanted and unwanted
are piling up in conversation and demanding my attention
i hear them but i seem more obsessed by a slice of past life
that keeps recurring and will not let me go

i wish you were here to help me finish this poem
i need your rhymes and insights, you who once asked me
to show you something i'd written
i never did
so
i hope you are patient and/or psychic
i wish i could find your poetry for sale on a stall
round the next corner and while we're at it why not mine too?

it is october and it is a national holiday

back then it was authentically autumn
i'd sit in a little square reading
while leaves fell and touched my shoulder
and time ticked by until we could meet again
so i don't remember any roses like the one here
in alcala de henares, the little city which
squares up to Madrid
nor yet like the roses whose petals drip
on every page in my copy of the collected poems
of juan ramon jimenez from huelva

but, in zaragoza during the fiestas del pilar
in another time and place
there was a song I remember
which went: dime tu nombre
y te hare reina en un jardin de rosas
and so let's say it there was love
that still walks with me today
in this country where we met

thank you very much ladies and gentlemen
and now I would like to invite our next poet to the stage

FRANCES BENNETT
Patchwork

The day spreads ahead like patchwork in the sun
Always work in progress the best bits the dull bits
Lily going for a walk in The House of Mirth
Samuel Beckett watching the fall of the Berlin wall
On TV in a nursing home
and saying, "C'est trop vite," it's too quick.
The lists and the unexpected, the podcast
On Thomas Hardy's poetry, the glimpse of alliteration
In Sir Gawain and the Green Knight.
Outside is clear and still with no wind
And the sun comes in onto the bed
Where the patchwork is laid, blue and green
From lockdown dressmaking, beloved clothes
Past their best, coloured cotton squares
Bought long ago because they appealed
All getting their chance to shine, to intertwine
And to surprise me while words from the radio
Play in the air above them.

ALEX BLABY
Emerald Path - The Boy

I'm standing beside a small plank of wood. It's weathered by what looks like many winter storms and bolted to two pieces of timber that have been driven into the ground. Rough grass is creeping out of the edges all around the legs, I'm sure I can see the odd insect in the gaps where the wood has been worn. I would have taken the time to sit upon this bench as I have the others, but it is currently occupied by a boy that can only just be entering his teens either this year or last. The bench isn't long enough for us both to rest and I don't want to disturb him as he is looking out into the distance. I'm not sure exactly what he is looking at or if he is waiting for the view to change. Currently there is a dense fog that destroys any visibility beyond the edge of the cliff about 2 metres in front. I'm looking to my left, then to my right. The fog seems to be forming a halo around my present location. I am keeping to the tradition of not looking back, but I can imagine the fog has engulfed us entirely where we stand.

If the young boy was standing we would be side by side. I am trying to align my perspective with his so I can gain an insight into what might have piqued his curiosity. There is nowhere for the eye to focus and it's hard to hold your gaze in a fixed position. I have turned to look at the boy hoping he will offer me some kind of clue, but he stays fixed looking ahead, his arms are crossed, not in such a way you would think he is angry, but as though he just doesn't know where else to put them.

It has crossed my mind to maybe ask him what he is doing here, and if he is even looking out for anything in particular, but it's so quiet right now the thought of making a single sound is just not an option. I should mention that the song I was able to hear when I first arrived has ceased entirely. I don't know when exactly, but between the crying lady and arriving at the cliff edge, all has fallen silent. I can't feel the breeze on my face anymore either, it is as though the air is standing entirely still, afraid to disturb the silence.

* * *

I have become quite lost in thought and didn't notice that the boy's position had changed. His left arm is raised, I am standing on his left by the way, and his finger is pointing outwards. He still looks quite relaxed, but it's clear he is trying to show me something. It might just be that he isn't showing me anything at all and is just pointing to guide his own focus to a particular spot.

    I am erring on the side of caution anyway and have tucked in a little behind his left shoulder to follow his line of sight. A flash! It was only brief and faint, but sure enough I saw it right where he was pointing. He has obviously been observing the spot for sometime and was expecting it. And again! It's like a tiny flicker of a candle, but so far in the distance that it must be quite the spectacle if you were nearby. The boy has dropped his arm now, he must realise that I have seen what he is seeing and I no longer need his guidance.

    He turns to me and I am expecting to see a smiling young face smug with the feeling that he was able to show me what he has been so patiently observing. But instead his face is one of complex emotions. I wasn't even aware before this moment that such a young face could manifest this level of complexity on its surface. Imagine the sadness of pinched lips holding back tears, the furrowed brow of confusion and yet the wide eyes of hope looking upwards. But of course he is looking upwards, for I am older and I should have the answers. I am standing by his side and was arriving just in time, ready to offer any guidance he requires, any concern that crosses his mind should be put to rest by those he looks up to. The longer I am holding his gaze, the narrower his eyes become. I am unsure as to what expression I am holding, but I can see that his expectation is slipping away. Whatever I am telling him, it isn't the answer he was looking for. He pulls himself away from my eye-line and fixes his sight to the ground in front of where he is sitting, it has become clear that he has lost hope. Not only in ever finding the purpose of the flash, but also in me. I should have brought him an answer, a conclusion and an end to his turmoil. But all I have brought him is disappointment.

    I feel compelled to stand with the boy for a while, I can't leave him as he is, but what am I to do? If I can't provide any answers then how can I fix things? He wants me to tell him what is ahead, but he has been observing for longer than I have, and I can only see what he sees. The more time I spend looking, the more I am becoming confused by the flash. It has no consistency, sometimes it is brighter than other times, and sometimes it flashes twice, or maybe three times. I am trying to count the seconds in between, but there appears to be neither rhythm or constant that it adheres to. Perhaps that is precisely the problem, we are both looking for something that isn't there. It could just simply be flashing for the sake of it. It might be because it has to for some purpose that neither of us have any business in knowing. It could just be a by-product of something that does have purpose, and we are trying to find a pattern in randomness.

    Without looking, I reach my right hand out and rest it upon his shoulder. I turn to look once again upon this tortured young soul. My sentiment has lifted his head out of its stoop and his eyes meet mine once more but this time something has changed. His expression is a clean slate, ready to mould into a form depending on the actions of the observer. I feel my cheeks pinch slightly, my head tilt and my shoulders shrug. He pauses for a moment before amusement fills his face for the first time since my arrival. He is laughing now. I notice over his shoulder that the fog is clearing, it almost looks like it's creating an archway to some kind of tunnel. Through the gap I can see more colour and vibrancy and the green of the pathway is illuminated once again. You might have noticed, as I have, that this means I am no longer going straight ahead, it seems my journey is continuing in
    another direction.

ALEX BLABY
The Long Tomorrow - 'Bed'

A small ashtray with silver paint peeling off its rim has a partially melted votive candle within its bowl. It sits upon a meagre wooden shelf which has lost the bracket at one end and is being supported by a collection of books, most of the spines are ripped or faded, their titles and authors lost to time. It is clear that the previous occupant considered them redundant as fountains of knowledge and that they would serve a much greater purpose as a bedside shelf. Through sunken bloodshot eyes this has been the only view for almost two days whilst Riley has slipped in and out of slumber.

The water offers a maternal rock of the cradle, the boat nudges slowly left, eternity passes, then right. A gentle creak of timber swelling here and there. Total darkness, all but the light of the moon slipping through the one porthole which isn't covered by a blanket. Its light offers a spotlight to the soft, linen plateau of the bed's surface, disrupted only by an indistinct mound of almost nothing. Gently rising, then deflating what seems to be a lifetime later, accompanied by the sound of a gentle sigh.

'What's the point?' is the theme of the evening. A crisis of discontent, despair and depression swell within grey matter, burning neurons until numb. Anaesthetic for the mind, but it offers no relief to this victim. The numbness only further deepens the pit.

What's the fucking point?

Any muscles are rendered useless by a sheer lack of will to move. And anyway, where is there to go? What is there to even do that serves purpose in this vast, unimaginable universe of illusionary purpose? There will never be anything that can encourage a hopeless wretch to escape from shackles wrought from a lifetime of self deprivation. The most minute passing thought becomes a soul devouring mare that labours upon the prisoner's chest. So unimaginably big and spiteful, cackling and snarling, pushing Riley deep into the bed until ribs could crack under the pressure. Not a single nerve spikes, no feeling, no pain, just, nothing. Momentary daydreams which would usually innocently rest a while are scrutinised, disembowelled and left for dead as the next victim dares manifest as a passing whimsy.

Two days spent in bed, what does that even mean? Days are just a measure of time and time serves no purpose. Sure humans seem to think it matters exactly how long it has been since the sun went down, and when it will come back up again, but really, what does it fucking matter? Days only exist so that we can measure how long we have left before we die. In this current state, Riley would revel in the thought of knowing how long that may be.

A mumble of defeat from beneath the covers.

"I need to piss."

Riley can bear it no longer, the battle of the mind can only ravage for so long before the bladder ensures that the human body, slave to its own biology, will succumb to its command.

A throw of the covers knocks the unlit candle off the shelf.

"Fuck sake."

A naked frame, laying exposed, emerging from hibernation, less rested than before. Eyes are sunken, gaping holes staring at the crack in the beam above the bed, this new scenery is cause for a pause. But only for a moment.

A bare chest begins to expand, lungs taking more air in one breath than they have over the course of two days. A dramatic exhale grapples the body, lifting it into a sitting heap. Bare feet touch the wooden floor briefly before quickly lifting again, a knee jerk reaction. It isn't that the floor is particularly cold, Riley is used to the temperature of living aboard a damp, draughty boat by now. It's the mere sensation of feeling that came as a shock. The touch of timber on the toes sent a pulse of life through this slither of being, albeit there is an air of indifference to the feeling returning, but it was an odd and unexpected recovery of sensation nonetheless. The second attempt, success. A slump and a shuffle forwards gets Riley to the door uneventfully. Muscle memory is subconsciously doing all the work in the pitch black, years of midnight dashes for relief means the use for candles at this hour is an unnecessary use of resources.

The trickling sound seems eternal as piss hits the surface of the moonlit glass, rippling along the creek from the starboard side of the bow, oscillating, but not severing, the bridge to the mirror world momentarily.

The two hollowed out cavities are now transfixed on the water, waiting until the disturbance has passed, allowing the pure reflection to return once more. Riley already knows what is going to happen next, already regretting the action that is going to be taken, what absolutely must be taken. A kind of self abuse and punishment for the wasted days, but also the only cure for the slump, the only thing that ever seems to work. While the mind is still battling on the deck as to whether or not it is a good idea, the body is already in mid air. The leap always seems to happen seconds before the logical part of the brain can tell the body what to do. It is as though there is a bug in the system, a rogue neuron that has a sole cognitive function, to know when a reboot is needed.

Much like getting out of bed, the feet are the first to feel, although this time there is no room for a knee jerk reaction. In a split second head to toe is immersed in a sensory overload, razorblades tear at every inch of the skin, firing ice cold responses to the brain, screams of pure anguish fire up in Riley's gut and manifest as bubbles in the aquatic sky. What goes down must come up. Riley breaches the divide between worlds and gasps for air, treading water, staring up at the dancing stars in the sky, the gaping eyes are widened by the immensity of what they behold. The brain is alert to a new kind of numbness, one that manifests by interaction with the physical world that will only ever be triggered by something so primitive as the survival instinct, there are no complex thoughts, no doubt in mind.

It is fucking cold, and Riley is fucking alive.

An extract from an upcoming book titled 'The Long Tomorrow'. A prophetic vision of the alternative lifestyles that will become a standard way of life as climate change prohibits the current conventions that we prescribe to. The future will require us to live more simple lives. Rekindling traditional practices, that have almost gone extinct in a mere generation, will be revived. A dystopia for some; A utopia for others.

ZAK BOWDEN
Another day another bolognese

Another day, another bolognese,
The perfect meal for my malaise,
Whence came this culinary craze?
Hypoglycaemia has me in a daze,
Another day, another bolognese.

'What's for tea for me this night?',
A question filling me with fright,
This distinct paucity of delight,
Owes itself to bags of mince,
And the sauce – which makes me wince,
Feeling pauper not the prince,
Plaster smile upon my face,
The rictus of a rat within the race,
Clear the table, set my place,
Another day another bolognese.

Oh most contemptible of comestibles,
Furthest thing from a festival,
Of flavour or indeed of fun,
'I loath to shit you from my bum,
To purge myself of what makes me glum',
I think as carrot lodges in my gum,
And this stodgy pasta that I chew,
Leaves me feeling black and blue,
Would've been better off with a stew…

Another day another fucking
Meal I wish I wasn't tucking in to-da-loo
I say to you, you piece of shit
The thing in life that makes me grit
my teeth the most
Haunting me like a ghostly demon
Straight from hell
I dunno from where the urge does swell
To carry on with this habit, oh… well,
Another day another bolognese.

LESLEY CHANDLER
Polly's Pancake Pantoum

Polly reads the tea leaves and the Tarot.
Her Yorkshire kitchen yields sugar-laden circles.
We drench them with the orange juices of sunshine and
we read the crinkly crêpe with abandon.

Jolly, fat and tipsy Polly.
Good at baking and babies Polly.
Resting her circles of golden love on the News of the World.
We eat, feast and *read* our Polly pancakes.

Her Yorkshire kitchen yields sugar-laden circles.
Jolly, fat and tipsy Polly.
We read the crinkly crêpes with abandon.
Good at baking and babies Polly.

Jolly, fat and tipsy Polly.
Resting her circles of golden love on the News of the World.
Good at baking and babies Polly.
We eat, feast and read our Polly pancakes.

We feast on hints of scandal in reverse.
We drench her golden circles with the orange juices of sunshine.
Resting her circles on sex, war and cures for baldness is
Polly, who reads the tea leaves and the Tarot.

A Pantoum is a Malaysian non-rhyming poem structure with a specific pattern of repetition.

INDIA CHILDS
Two old men on a train from London to…? or 'The Philosophers'

Paddington Station, 1pm.
Mostly clean, though
the smell of fried food,
dried sweat atop wilting
notes of perfume, lingers.
Pigeons pecking everywhere,
streaks of purple and green wreathing their primly tucked wings,
pecking madly at dashing feet, unseeing eyes
another train pulls in
the departure board flickers, so many tiny squares of electro-blue black,
mustard lines melting into
each other, reflected in the yellow tinge of
the glazed-over faces,
emerging onlookers grouping from
nowhere, suddenly everywhere.
Scratching noses through masks.
Mick seeks Rick out in
the dense sea
shuffling his sidelong two step,
two steaming costa mugs,
english breakfast tea,
a strong black, another milky grey,
the hot lids biting at his broken lines, edged onto the base of his hands.
Mick's whole body is a broken line,
end of the line affair.
He gets away with pushing through
due to his hobble, the stutter in
his step, the fumbling for his ticket
as the barrier monitor grabs his bags.
Other passengers on the platform are sympathetic, clearly
not Londoners, hailing tourists in a cold,
unseeing-stupid-pigeon-eyed city.

The carriage. Confusion as
the announcement details a
mistake. Nine carriages whittled down to five.
Other trains from Exeter for those heading to Bristol are advised.
Humid, people pushing down their masks now
to check their dry mouths are still there, that
they didn't drop them in the gap
between the train and
the platform.
Corridor quaking, small sounds of shuffling as
the train pulls away.
No seats left. Social distancing a dearly departed
friend of convenience, of
circumstance.
Rick's cold, actually. It's very cold. He
watches the young people opposite shrug
off jackets and smirks. It's
so simple. Things now.
He's so old, so observationary of
the world's young, where everything they do
is endearing, worth smiling about.
He's a father to everyone under thirty,
watching as if their baby shuffles slowly
across the floor, trying to walk and
falling again, gormless, ungracious. So
silly in everything.
The girl opposite catches his eye
marks his mind as one of disdain
and turns away, blushing, not sure why she feels
so ashamed.
Mick and Rick both enjoy these powers obtained
through age, small moments
where others assert themselves on their behalf,
every prolonged, passing instance of eye contact
interpreted as a stifling incident of unflinching judgement.
But it isn't that. It's just, Mick and Rick both are bored.
That is all.

You know this route, it isn't
as half as long as it would have been twenty years ago.
Yes, yes. Do you remember when you'd have to walk from the station
to a bus stop, then walk a mile to
another after that first bus left, and then eventually
get to where you wanted to go.
Crazy, that. Shaking of heads. Crazy.
Was that really twenty years ago?
Oh, not even I reckon it was forty, now
I really think about it. I always think
less time has passed than the amount that has. Strange. Terrible.
Shaking of heads again.
Do you want half my ham and pickle chap?
(Huffs) depends. Branston?
No, Myrtles homemade.
You said that last time and it turned out to be a cheap knock-off,
plastic In flavour.
No no no. I wasn't going to take a packed lunch but
She insisted. New batch, fresh just
the day before yesterday.
Beat of silence, sacred as a vow. Speed racketing the glass
a single puff of wind from a slightly opened window many seats away.
Munching in a sombre solidarity, in a union recalling their lost youth.
A strong smell of ancient onion, disgusted
and contemptuous looks concealed in slithers,
of exposed, crescent moon expressions.
You know. A loud swallow, a belch neither acknowledges.
I never told you this, but I'll say now, it being so long ago.
I kissed Myrtle once. At that parish youth dance, you
recall the one, all the multi-coloured balloons.
Over-eighteens only. Before you were both going
steady, of course.
I never! Wow. She's not told me that. Always says how
handsome you are though, how trim. A dry chuckle
adding further to the humidity, the surrounding vapour.
Makes sense now I suppose.
They prattle on, their conversations
overlapping like water between rocks,

puddles of placid, artless communication
expanding into the cracks, seeping. Ancient ring marks
being stamped onto with new recyclable coffee cups
scattered across the flimsy fold out trays.
Everything here
is a small construction affair, prone to obliteration.
The seven-quid sushi bowls only justified
by tube-tired, fatigued minds, damp cardboard
crumpled into the gaps between seats,
dog-eared like the dense books other
passengers pretend to read. And it amounts
to nothing, none of it, only a busier bin at the end station,
where everyone's rubbish has touched each other
for far longer than anyone would like to think of
where the food sweat of leftovers, clinging to wrappers,
to crumpled crisp packets, is its own little structure
built from the remnants of so many others
of strangers that didn't look twice at each other
but amidst this fray, create a colony
a green and brown mould microcosm,
a better version of society.
And Mick doesn't like to bin things until he gets home,
not as a rule, but as a habit. His idle hands layer foil
and cling film into dense dusty terrains of crumbs and
plastic, lining the inside of his coat pockets. Some he
keeps hold of longer than others, because
they offer him a strange sort of comfort. When he
looks at all those young faces and feels fear,
for a reason that escapes him, he reaches for
those balls of rubbish like they might help him.
Rolling between his thumb and index finger,
And then Rick, who always notices after a while,
asks why what have you got there?
And he wakes up, as if from a dream, and shrugs it off
a mumbled 'oh just fiddling', and takes another bite
of his sandwich, stray pickle on his lip, a subconscious
note to self to save all the mess for later.
You remember back when we took

that round trip, four-hundred miles
to St Ives, just us and Dave who was bloody useless
what with all his toilet breaks and talk of his missus
oh yes. Yes, I remember. And how sloshed we
all were throughout most of it, how we played a gig at that
pub Dave booked God knows where, and we almost got thrown off
stage and he punched the bar manager after.
It was a night to remember
A dry chuckle, a fistful of peanuts, crusted with salt.
Dave. It's a shame he knocked it when he did.
Yes, even though he was useless. He
was a laugh.
They can't look at each other so turn to passengers
opposite, chortling loudly
on other anecdotes, tutting at all the people
clinging to their phones,
at all the millennials torturing themselves
drip-fed desire on their screens,
reminders that they are still alone.
Crazy how you see all these young people today on their
devices and such. You remember Paul, I do
like it was yesterday. How when his old man collapsed
(the heart attack), and we had to call an ambulance,
running two miles to the phone box only to scream
ourselves hoarse at the queue, the young lovers waiting,
the gentlemen placing their bets on the races, or selling
and we pummelling through, and Paul was sweating,
but so white in the face, no colour left, drained
and in the end it didn't matter, he still died
and the whole village, who as we dialled the number,
held its breath, resumed its dull chatter once again.
All bets placed to honour Ted's good name.
Nothing has really changed.
Nothing? Everything. Everything has changed.
Mick and Rick, who so often find
comfort in each other,
the only ones left alive
in their old friendship groups numbers

do not agree on this. Because Mick,
he's making plans, every day
thinking about the next step, about the after
which doesn't scare him as much as it used to.
Because Mick, he sees it everywhere, at the train stations
at the traffic lights, at the signals that tell you to go
left or instead, right. And
he loses his balance being told
what to do, in the places he doesn't recognise, where
everything feels new. And he's being replaced, he
can see it's true. The generation below are catching up,
and they know better than he tries to.
All he wants
is Rick, to remind him even if he's ready to leave it
that he had a life and he goddamn fucking lived it
every single fucking bit of it.
And the heat of the carriage, it gets to him, for the first time
the proximity of bodies, huddled up the aisle, rigid over
suitcases, rigour-mortis in the passengers enslaved to time
to the two hours left to go before they reach the
end of the line.
How the pins and needles ache
is all that satisfies them that they are still awake
but that these old men nattering
deserve a good shake. Spinning sentences
that are loud and loathsome,
causing headaches.
And Mick takes off his coat, and Rick raises a brow,
because Rick likes living still in the now,
but feels more comfortable because he sees
patterns where Mick sees plots,
where everyone pretends to be something they're not.
And maybe it's because Rick has grandkids that
he loves, he's got ties to the new age, he's got
plans, and Mick has nothing but nostalgia
and an envy that leaves him estranged,
because he has a mindset on life that can't really change.
But they don't fight. This is the one thing they can't pretend

this is the thing that is theirs, the thing they learnt
that wasn't endorsed by everyone else's version of
what growing up is supposed to be. They know
that fighting solves nothing, so they leave it be
and prattle on, order from the lunch trolley more tea,
and raise their voices louder, looking out longingly
at the part of the journey where the tracks meet the sea
hoping wherever they're going it's where they are
both meant to be.

JAMES CROFTSON
Richer in the morning

The Chancellor will open his red briefcase and explain:
His economy is stalling, and it's our fault in the main;
We must have been such lazy little boys and girls again,
But - not to worry - for a 'new idea' is spawning.
He'll flood the banks with money, in the form of more QE,
And if it doesn't trickle down into society,
Then he'll balance up the books (by 'redefining GDP'):
And we'll all be richer in the morning.

The ministers will gather, to debate and disagree,
On the reasons for the failure of our growth economy.
The elephant in the room that they all will fail to see
Is the one they for years have been adorning,
Where the thing that matters most is annual growth of two percent -
Not the lack of bank deposits notes are 'sposed to represent -
But if wealth is just a measure of 'resources we have spent',
Then, yes of course, we'll be richer in the morning.

   And it doesn't really matter if we will the last tree
   Or haul the last fish up in the net.
   It all helps to bolster our economy,
   And, as long as we forgot about debt,
   Then we'll all be richer in the morning.

A 'strong and stable government' the 'majority' croon,
While three fifths of the country sing a very different tune;
It doesn't look like happening anytime soon,
As another rift in Number Ten is forming.
Lobbyists are wined and dined: campaign groups are a pest,
The population's ageing and the NHS is stressed;
At least our representatives 'all did their jolly best
To ensure we'd be richer in the morning'.

Our workshops and factories are gathering dust.
As we import more than export we depend more on our trust

That our service-based economy will stop us going bust,
Yet we talk of a 'golden era' dawning.
We built our nation on industrial flair,
Then shipped the jobs to China 'cos they're cheaper over there
Now we tell each other proudly, as we cut each others' hair,
That we'll all be richer in the morning.

    And it doesn't really matter if we will the last tree
    Or haul the last fish up in the net.
    It all helps to bolster our economy,
    And, as long as we forgot about debt,
    Then we'll all be richer in the morning.

Taxpayers' money will be used to buy advice
From dodgy auctioneers who want to keep a low price:
They want to have our cake and eat it and then take an extra slice -
Are we all too blind to see the warning?
What the left hand offers, the right hand retracts:
Higher wages? Higher VAT and Income Tax.
All we have to do is trust the bankers have our BACS,
And we'll all be richer in the morning.

Social inequality continues to increase,
There's less and less funding for firemen and police,
More and more kids are getting more and more obese,
And we spend our days wilfully scorning.
Financial anxiety is becoming quite a force,
As more and more marriages are citing, in divorce,
Thank God the Chancellor will keep us on this course:
Because we'll all - be - richer - in - the - morning.

JAMES CROFTSON
Simple Pleasures

Simple pleasures for simple minds, with modern measures so ill-defined,
Seem to be derogatory: used to imply inferiority;
   Uninformed translation - conceptual relegation -
   To obsolescence soon they'll be confined:
And simple pleasures, for simple minds, will be sidelined.

Simple pleasures for simple minds, in high opinions: 'un-refined',
Seeming lost and ineffectual, far too far below the intellectual.
   Seeking something grander, we uphold the propaganda
   That simplicity and cost are intertwined,
And simple pleasures, for simple minds, are hard to find.

    We worry what the future holds, hoping not to take a fall:
    We wonder what brings happiness, but we don't understand at all,
    The simple pleasures that simple minds desire to find.

Overstated, underlined, orchestrated just behind
Expensive taste, expansive waste: wrapped in plastic and
in my sub-conscience placed:
   I feel I am caught between the wheels in the 'brand machine':
   My hopes and fears are re-aligned;
And simple pleasures, for simple minds, are undermined.

    We worry what the future holds, holding not to take a fall,
    We wonder what brings happiness, but we don't understand at all,
    The simple pleasures that simple minds desire to find.

KIM CROFTSON
I do not dress to impress

I do not dress to impress.

My consciousness is not with you in mind.

I consider the hands that tied the knots of the threads. The hands ripped to shreds. I consider the mind driven to distraction with monotony. I consider the heart broken by the 84-hour working week. Broken because the clothes I wear, this top I choose, is my desire. *It is my right* to look good. *It is my right* to fit in. *It is my right*, to believe that what others think of my appearance matters more.

I do not dress to impress.

My consciousness is not with you in mind.

I can have what I want because I can, because the money I earn speaks louder than other expressions of exchange. It shouts louder than the money which quietly, reluctantly drips in to the broken hands that skilfully make. I can have what I want because I can. Because I have the right to walk free, to clothe myself without possessing any textile skill.

I do not dress to impress.

My consciousness is not with you in mind.

Yet, I still walk on those stricken hands without hearing the cry of pain. I still walk over the distracted mind without a care beyond myself. I still scatter the shards of the shattered heart without any understanding of the toil.

I do not dress to impress.

My consciousness is not with you in mind.

KIM CROFTSON
Bus stop

Sat legs crossed at the bus stop
watching the rain cradle the pane
She asks if I need a light.
Her eyes directed, pierced, chipped at the cracks
I looked back, empty.

"I don't smoke"

Early evening was drawing in steely grey lines
while heavy drops disturbed, redefined, fell in time,
messed with shape and form.

Then she spoke

"Life is hard don't you think?"
I shivered as the words draped on the mist of her breath drifted
I pulled my collar tight, shifted in my seat
I wanted to say go away
but my lips quivered
frozen in the wreck, the confusion and disillusion
that this life was not what I had planned.
I gave a reluctant nod. A full agreement
unspoken

Life is hard!

Sat at the bus stop
watching the rain cradle the pane
stark headlights streaked through the dusk
still no bus

when she asks "What if?"

The words tumbled heavily, scattered autumn sediment
crashed through my ears, disturbing hardened sentiments

of hopelessness
I looked up. Glimpsed the flicker reflected in her eyes
her smile warm and wise
and I sighed, "what if?"

What if this was not all that there could be,
all that there should be, all that there would be
What if there was more beside….

When she clarified
"This Light is bright inside. He serves as my guide
when life is dark and dense
when nothing seems to make sense
I stop.
Breath in the Light of the world.
Breathe out His light in my world."

Then she paused.
My tight chest unfurled and I heard.
gentle on her lips, a name whispered,
drips, viscous, sweet,

"Jesus"

The truth broke over me,
dawned around me
Surrounded my listless being.
The dark long shadows fleeing as if in
a time lapse view of the dawning, radiant sun

I am undone.

Jesus the light of the world is come!

Sat legs crossed at the bus stop
watching the rain cradle the pane
warm bulbs spark between bricks
attempting to stem the slick flow of night

a futile protest for the waning dusk
still no bus

When she asks "Do you need The Light?"

Her eyes directed, pierced, chipped at the cracks,
I looked back, empty.

yet I smiled,
sight restored, reassured

This life is hard.
I gave a willing nod, a full agreement
unspoken

This life was not what I had planned,
but I understand a little more
that His Light tells the whole story, strikes to the core
works to restore and make new

He illuminates, pulls focus, edifies our lives
surprises us with new ways

Stays.

Do I need The Light?

KIM CROFTSON
Wildlight

The expectant star raises our gaze
beyond the here and now -
drawing us far in to the distant echo of time gone
renders our praises for the years to come.

Its radiant invitation captivates our senseless being,
Shatters numbness

breaks in.
breaks out.
breaks over.

Finds us, leads us to discover the beauty in the being
Such Beauty in The Being!

Fervently search the firmament,
seek the way.

Uncover Presence inescapable
Capable of covering us, able and vulnerable

Baffled by thoughts innumerable -
pursue the wildlight, impenetrable and unbearable

Arrive.

Find delicate grace, unfathomable.
Stay a while.
Rest,
the child is here

ablaze with timeless hope.

ALAN CUMMINGS
The Band Has Split Up

Here is some news of interest
I just sacked my guitarist
We've been together a very long time
Ever since I wrote my first song
In 1971

To be honest, he wasn't very good then
To be honest he's never been quite up to the mark
I just didn't like to say anything
Because he was me
And I didn't want to upset myself

It's a bit of a cliché, isn't it
The band splitting up I mean
But splitting up with myself after all these years
Has been particularly emotional
I really didn't know how to explain myself
To myself

It's not your chords, I said
Or your dexterity from fret to fret
But I was lying of course
And he knew
Because I was him and he was me

Why are you really doing this he asked himself
With a tear in our eye and a pale grey plectrum
between our fingertips
Tell me the truth. Is there someone else?
Don't be silly, I said
I just need a little time to myself

But I am yourself he pleaded and
Tired of all this
I locked him in the cupboard

So here I am at the Moth and the Moon
Having left myself bereft at home
And now my music's locked away
All my words can come out to play

ALAN CUMMINGS
Daddies Dancing

Daddy longlegs everywhere
They scare my wife but they don't scare me
She says they're far too spider-like
While I just see fragility

She wishes they were all quite dead
All scattered legs and broken wings
But I see them as fairy folk
The late September weather brings

She contemplates a massacre
I visualise a fairy ball
Where long-legged fairy daddies dance
To prove who dances best of all

And what I'd really like to know,
While daddy longlegs congregate,
Where do mummy longlegs go?
And do they
Sensibly
Just wait?

ALAN CUMMINGS
Love Lost in Fourteen Lines

I know where once I made you laugh out loud
More often now I make your rivers cry
Where once I watched you soar above the crowd
The wings I gave no longer help you fly

No more the words to ease the ache you feel
No more the skills to quicken your heart's beat
You see now just the turning of a wheel
And links of steel that bind your restless feet

I sought to tell why still I'm at your side
When I no longer seem enough for you
I search but heart and reason so collide
That true turns into false and false to true

Perhaps for me the scent of love remains
In memories that look to you like chains

ALAN CUMMINGS
The Epitaph

Before I crossed my own sad bridge of sighs
I made a friend with mastery of stone
I told him of my luck and loss in life
And begged an epitaph when I was done

So now he stands with chisel in his hand
And measures out the words I wished to see
While thinking of the tales that I had told
And forgiving, as he did, my vanity

On being a swimmer and diver

I told him smiling how it felt to swim
With sleek and swift and deadly barracuda
And how the gentle, private octopus
Admonished me as unwelcome intruder

I told him how it felt to stroke with care
The stingray sleeping in the yellow sand
And how the playful spotted puffer fish
Would twist and turn to dodge my reaching hand

I told him of the grey shark's icy eye
"As close to me as you are now" I said
And how I hung in Indian Ocean blue
To see the distant, graceful hammerhead

So as he carves, at my request, this stone
And thinks about the voyages I sailed
He wonders at my stipulated text
"Here I lie, rock and roll star, brackets, failed"

On being a restorer of paintings

I told him how I learned to bring to life

Fine portraits of forgotten great and good
Neglected, cold and damp, 500 years
Still clinging to their pigment, linen, wood

I set to right their gold and silk and lace
Embroidery as fine as spiders spin
A million tiny strokes of cadmium
Alizarin, viridian and tin

The kings of England sought my help to shine
Great poets to my trusty easel came
Philosophers and military men
And scientists and lovers of great fame

So as he carves, at my request, this stone
And contemplates the skills my work entailed
He wonders at my stipulated text
"Here I lie, rock and roll star, brackets, failed"

On being an academic

I told him how in time I changed my course
And took a turn down Academia Street
In universities of great repute
Where art and science I'd persuade to meet

The mathematics of the Parthenon
The resonance of fragile elastanes
The laser scans of ancient polychrome
The ivory and bone and peptide chains

And when with pride Professor I became
And fast ascended to the Management
I did my best to hang on to my soul
And nurture students in their own ascent

So as he carves, at my request, this stone
And sees me in my College robes regaled

He wonders at my stipulated text
"Here I lie, rock and roll star, brackets, failed"

On being a songwriter and performer

I told him last of ventures on the stage
In bands that now seem blessed with stupid names
In grimy, slimy music pubs and clubs
Elation here and there shot down in flames

But the songs, I said, would simply crystallise
From somewhere in my head or in the air
And this was where my joy would never wane
The confluence of words and notes to share

A record deal secured with Polydor
A tour in Europe, triumph in Berlin
I heard myself just once on Radio One
And then I watched the clichéd cracks begin

So as he carves, at my request, this stone
And sees my disappointment quite unveiled
He understands at last my stipulated text
"Here I lie, rock and roll star, brackets, failed"

MIKE DEMPSEY
No worries, Dad

No worries dad
You can stop worrying now
You don't have to give it one seconds thought
The fence is all fine, we got there on time
And it don't matter about the shoes that you bought

No worries dad
You can stop worrying now
You can close your eyes and put those worries to bed
The forecast is dry, you don't have to try
To keep earning a living in the cold and the wet

No worries dad
You can stop worrying now
There's no need for you to worry any more
The windows are clean, the lawn is all green
And nobody cares what's behind the front door

No worries dad
You can stop worrying now
What's left of Eden will disappear any day
You won't need a mower, it's concreted over
And the world is completely fucked up anyway

No worries dad
You can stop worrying now
You don't have to worry that I won't say my prayers
It's God bless Mammy, and God bless Daddy
And take away the worries that always was theirs

And tell me again that they rest in your arms
And tell them I'm sorry for the times I hurt them

There's no worries dad
For the time that you had

There's no worries now no toil or burden

No worries dad
You can stop worrying now
No one will misunderstand your intentions
The bills are all paid, the beds have been made
The sum of your transgressions, too little to mention

MIKE DEMPSEY
Halo

Although he was ordinary and a little bit grey
Nigel woke up with a halo one day
It was there in the mirror as he sat on the bed
Something round and shiny just over his head

He turned to his wife who by now had awoke
"Is this you playing some kind of a joke?
Tell me the truth say yes or say no
Am I losing my mind or is that a halo"

She rubbed sleep from her eyes to see what was what
"Perhaps its the light shining off your bald spot"
But as she looked closer she had to agree
A halo was what the thing seemed to be

She asked what could have caused such a strange happenstance
"Did you dream something crazy by any chance
Like seeing miracles or priests with stigmata
I told you not to eat that late cheese and tomato

I don't want to seem like I'm making a fuss
But phenomena like this shouldn't happen to us
It should be good people or maybe a saint
And someone like that - you definitely ain't

See how it goes, just give it an hour
Perhaps it'll wash off when you go in the shower"
But it didn't wash off, in fact it shone more
'Till he felt like he couldn't go out of the door

He told work he was sick when he phoned his boss Jed
And made an appointment with the doctor instead
He got funny stares as he walked up the street
So he kept his head down and just looked at his feet

He walked all the way and avoided the bus
To spare consternation and a terrible fuss
The doctor's receptionist started to snigger
She couldn't imagine a problem much bigger

The doctor was clever he'd been to college
But said that a halo was outside of his knowledge
He tried grabbing it but his hand went straight through
He was at a loss as to what he could do

"I know of a doctor whose chief occupation
Is to find the root cause of strange manifestations"
He phoned in advance and wrote down the address
And told Nigel it's free on the NHS

So he went straight there – he thought he'd better
The sign said Parker and then lots of letters
"I'm Doctor Parker but just call me Ron
My friends call me Nosey but thats just for fun"

Ron asked many questions "Do you catch bugs?
Do you smoke fags or take any drugs?
Do you work hard or are you a skiver?"
Nigel said "No I'm a fork lift truck driver"

"Do you drink liquor, are you alcohol free
Is your BMI approximately where it should be?
Do you talk to plants, do you have much good luck?
I wonder have you ever been thunderstruck?

Are you psychic, do you have ESP?"
He took samples of blood and samples of wee
"Nigel we must get to the bottom of this
What thinks your wife, what thinks your kids?"

"We don't have children. it's just me and her"
At that moment another angle to Ron did occur
"Are you a virgin, it could hold the key?"

"Mind your own business, that's for my wife and me"

Ron gave a frown he had no more ideas
There was nothing in the books he'd been reading for years
"I think in all fairness you could do much worse
Than to take yourself off down the road to the church"

The vicar was old and had a bad cough
He was a conservative man of the cloth
He didn't see change as a necessity
And thought the halo a fashion accessory

"Get out of my church and don't you come back
Wearing a stupid thing like that
Are you one of these crazies from a weird sect
Don't you have one single ounce of respect"

Word spread around - nobody had seen
A man with a halo where his hat should have been
The papers got wind and thought we'll make a ton
So they put poor Nigel up there on page one

The thought of publicity put him into a sweat
And then it got worse with the internet
Many debated this unusual drama
And sought the advice of the Dalai Lama

Who was reluctant his opinion to bring
So told them he thought it a Catholic thing.
Someone tried phoning the Pope in Rome
But was told that His Holiness wasn't at home

Theologians debated and wrote many a book
About things in scripture perhaps overlooked
An art historian who's name was Kenneth
Decided he would put in his two penneth

"It doesn't actually mean you're holy" he said

"Just cause a halo is over your head
It's only in paintings this form of apparel
So you can easily tell the good from the rabble

In my expert opinion I have to say
It's unlikely the holy walked around that way"
Podiatrists had notions that they thought quite neat
And turned the idea right up on it's feet

"Instead of studying where the halo is found
Lets look at where his legs touch the ground"
They prodded his heels and counted his toes
They washed his feet with a high pressure hose

But podiatrists and theologians could not agree
To anything that happen below the knee
Because of the internet, now fame he could boast
He soon caught the attention of a chat show host

Who offered Nigel an unrefusable fee
To come on to Saturday night TV
They said to be honest and emotions don't hide
So he talked about the time when his mummy died

And about the trampoline on which he loved to play
And how he just couldn't jump the sadness away
And he jumped even when it started to rain
'Cause he wanted that happy feeling again

Instead of clouds that seemed almost black
And he prayed and he prayed that she might be sent back.
But that didn't happen despite all his love
So he stopped thinking about things like heaven above

There was a song out then by a bloke called Ray
It said "Everything's beautiful in it's own way"
And he tried to understand what's good and what's bad
And all the mixed up feelings he suddenly had

He said that his story was sad but daft
And a man held a sign up and the audience laughed
The chat show host said I must ask you true
Why has this halo appeared over you

Nigel shrugged and sighed, not for the first time
"I tell you, your guess is as good as mine
But I've been thinking since all this occurred
I've listen to people with many a word

Some say they're experts and know all the answers
But half the time they're just out and out chancers
They'll talk of science, they'll talk of tradition
They'll sit you right down and make you listen

They'll tell you white's black, and blue can be red
But none of them know why this thing's on my head
If I had a query or was a bright spark
Would it be a lightbulb or question mark?

Perhaps its a sign due to faith that I lack
That somehow someone up there wants me back
There's so much beauty to see all around
Yet so many people to bring you down

There's joy in a father and love in a mother
Yet terrible things we still do to each other
There's only one more thing that I've left to say
It's thanks for the money - I'll be on my way

That is how it is and why? Cause I say so
And one morning I just woke up with a halo"
Nigel got up and stood proud and tall
Then went home with his money and halo and all

And if there's a moral by way of a closure
It's wake up with a halo and not a hangover

MAC DUNLOP
untitled (excerpt)

    I need this out of my life right now. Angie slumped over the table her, hands stretched across the tablet screen. Overcome with the new enhancement app – trying it on five stars straight out of the box wasn't the best idea as it turned out – she wept onto the pixels. They magnified in her teardrops, each with a tiny rainbow glow around them like minute crystals. The drones flew everyday now, low too, with impunity, ever since all traces of small arms fire had been extinguished. Back home, the government hailed the rubbled city as a sign of vanquished foes. Hospitals and anything else worth having in an urban environment were reduced to piles of tangled steel and concrete. The days of having work and having a life had all shut down. Greyness coated everything. Lungs coughed as soon as they cried out. Pressed against a cheek, the tablet slept beneath her face. Her pulse twitched under her closed eyes. She counted. Stress was the killer here, the pen pushing stress of matching data inputs to images. AI's apes; the code filing clerks working from home for the price of guaranteed signal. Neotelligence would take over from them all soon. Even now it could probably be more her than her. Then the machine thinking could be planted under the skin of her wrist and she'd just drop back into the viral load and let her screen face take over. They'll still be my tears, she rallied, feeling the child shift inside. A little kick was uncomfortable and the shifting inside got her sitting back up. Wiping the screen with the cuff of her shirt, she stared at the blank glass and her reflection in it, wondering what might come next.

    She was sure she was pregnant with a monster, but no one believed her. Against the background of green screen relish tinted hand paint, a sweep of drone footage collapsed under his/her weight. Sitting in the fantasy as if squashing dreamlike metaphors, they were angled on one side of the truth or so, as witnesses mounted each virtual sniper's favourite spot. Waiting for the cavalcade, baton twirling tassel skirted fancy booted knee steppers controlled the pace and rhythm of the marching band hypnotically. Bus tour mystical. A tiny amount of words make charming lyrics, even if they interrupt the one guy against the world fantasy shit. Wishing only for the kind of thing only money can get you out of. Super pac me, dump me, portray the hip replacement face of the future on my campaign bus just get me a seat at the table.

A magpie crested the mummified pimento bush. Sand as countless as stars, the universe a beach for unimaginable giants. Human conceit made war inevitable and starvation a necessity. Cultural anorexia voted malnourished ideologies into office and paraded them on technically illegal t shirts at virtual protests. Everything was naughty all at once, dark and in that way beautifully terrifying - imagine a thousand deaths then imagine a thousand more. The what to do with the bodies alone, imagine, even without repeating. It all came dancing in the broken passenger jets that cut through the air one after another like a spilled loaf of sliced bread. You could hear the fear in the contrails, they were already almost pink with the impending crash. Velocity destroyed every disintegrating piece as they dissolved into crumbs and began floating in the surrounding pockets of air.

They ripped the jeans from her at the checkout, saying what was she thinking, who was this he bloke whom she said would pay? Who was this he she never wanted to be? The plastic carded 5 o'clock shadow of a shrivelled penis poking from its pube curled nest. Where did the brambles come from? Next door, or were they real? The birds that queued for the ceramic bowl full of water, the birds picking through the autumn birch leaves. How were they imagined? How the sparrow hawk had laid its prey to rest, remember? Its arched back so peaceful and flat as if readied for a steady stream of mourners to pass by paying their last respects. Like it might rise again, its innards having been temporarily borrowed for some thought experiment. She loved him though, so said nothing as they searched her. They left her without water, they accused her of endangering her unborn. They locked her up and threw away the key.

Once, lives had personas all their own. A simple tremolo, a vibe of who wants some more? There was only so much of that. It had finally began receding from the bottom and making its way to the top slowly, like an old lava lamp.

Rust itched beneath her skin. It was in a dream that she saw it, orange bright against her, owning everything a few layers down. Everything. Eyebrows, breasts, bellybutton. The child wasn't safe. No hiding where the police had gone. Her age was a relative opinion. It would be no use as evidence in court.

MAC DUNLOP
Time to Go

"Let's go" he said, moving the chess piece forward. Too many words made up the statement, they left no room for thought. He undid his skin suit and wandered around the anatomy class, pretending to admire various charcoal sketches being generated by the childlike robots. Overnight there had been a bomb storm and everyone had moved further south as suggested by the Junta. Those too ill were unplugged skin-wise and left to dessicate in the wind. Upstairs a series of words were being used to slice bread into prepared meals. The museum kitchen was required to hold demonstrations of various historic methods of preparing food. The time may come when it can only be consumed by mouth once more.

In the dream my skin was having, it saw an entire world of art being flooded. The curator was very apologetic, as they often are in dreams. Helpless and uprooted. A book was being tossed into the waves by children playing on the new shoreline left by recent floods. The only way out of the water was to clamber over them. The kids were like large respiring stones or slowly scrambling sea turtles. Someone in a see-through canoe had beached on top of them and was taking pictures. To try to get a better shot, they had thrown all the life jackets overboard. A giant sketch made of cardboard had been framed on an outside wall. It depicted a breast-feeding mother and child. It soaked up water from the outpourings of the roof above. It sagged into a wet towel before falling off and disintegrating. The curator apologised again, sorry they couldn't fix it, couldn't make it right, it was not what the artist had intended.

The curator bit themself then swallowed continuously, gnawing at their own bones while still fawning forgiveness. "Let that be a lesson" someone said. Rockets streamed overhead. In two places on either side of the world, festival goers were being mown down with automatic weaponry. On one hand, the shooter was alone in a hotel with a telescopic sight. On the other, a group of khaki clad caterpillars wielding Kalashnikov rip-offs rode in on armoured mushroom clouds. "We're just getting started" one of them said.

It was time to go.

CHLOÉ EATHORNE
Midnight Bike Rides with You

Skipping stones with you
Under the pink moon
We fly through the ebony night
Two white birds soaring
Handlebars clasped, taking flight.
The scent of jasmine permeates the air
Electric, our laughter chimes
The soft salty breeze waltzes as
We trace the sand, and I feel your heart beside mine.
As bright and as full as the moon
Solid and soft,
Tender and true,
Like the birdsong that tangles
Through the seaweed.
We talk through all hours of the night
Each one an intricate metal
Clockwork, no half crescents here.
In your eyes,
I am transported
To sage green sun dappled forests
The light dissolving all that is wrong
With the world
Leaving only
Joy,
Peace,
Serenity
As green and verdant as the chlorophyll
Catching the morning light,
It Ignites
Something
You cannot condense into words.

LAUREN GAUGE
Poison Ivy

Personified ricin.
You lacing
my thoughts pacing,
mind hazy
feeling crazy,
playbacks phase in.

Pulse racing
Checking me out
Spacing me out
Nerves hiding
Hands sliding
Devil inside
I confide in
Alcohol plied
Confidence high
Taking pride in
you smiling
Compliments flying
Tongues faking
Love making
Consequences piling
Kiss and goodbye-ing
Hugging and kissing
Waving and missing
Days passing
Fingers dialling
Mouth drying
Awake lying
Dilemma peaks
No sleep
I'm trying
Lonely sacrificing
I'm justifying

You,
my personified ricin.
Downward spiralling
Eyes dry from
Come down crying
Addict dying
For more highs n'
Rollers rights
Gamble long nights
To get sight of
Your dark delights
My endless plight
What if?
You won't
I might
Guilty fight
Just to kiss you goodnight
Hold you tight

It can't be wrong
If it makes me write
Like I've been read my last rights
It can't be wrong
If it feels this right
Shines a light so bright
Into my crooked little life
Makes me feel alive
It's primal
Fuck it
It's survival

VINCENT GOULD
Let there be art

In the beginning
The earth was formless and void
And the Great Administrator
Came down from her office on the second floor
And she looked at the void
And she said,
Let this void be filled with arts-related content
And she looked at the content
And it was good

And she said,
Let there be light
And four hundred energy-saving lightbulbs were fitted in place
And she looked at the light
And it was good

And she said,
Let there be an eatery
And many staff were employed
On zero-hours contracts

And she said,
Let there be art
And it was
For anything she declared did come to pass

And she looked at the art
And it was good

And then she looked at the artists
And she said,
There are definitely improvements that could be made here
Let us make artists in our own image
And they shall be called
Workshop Leaders and Facilitators

And there shall be
Endless poetry workshops
One for each day of the week
And they shall stretch unto eternity

And after this time,
Many lesser administrators came to her
Saying,
Let us benefit from your wisdom
For many artists want to speak to us
And we do not know what to say to them
So she gathered them around her
And told them,
If an artist comes to you for help,
Do not give him the desires of his heart
Instead, place many obstacles in his way
So that he may know
The true hardship
Of the art world

And all were astonished by the wisdom of her words

VINCE GOULD
In real time

This is happening
In real time
I am the data
You are the drive

Take a snapshot
With your eye
Store it in your memory
For another time

Record the audio
With your ear
The beat
Is here

You may not be able
To skip
Or double back
And see what you've missed

But
If you let it hit
It will be you
And you
Will be it

Like it
With your hands
Share it
With your mouth
Subscribe
In your philosophy

This is happening
In real time
I am the data
You are the drive

PAUL HACKETT
Gone but not forgotten

She did not know what day it was,
what month or even the year,
It must have been a scary place,
confused with so much fear.

Did not know where she was,
or where she was going to go,
did not remember the names,
of those she used to know.

Did not know what season it was,
even if it was Christmas Day,
could not really remember much,
or think of things to say.

She'd smile when she would see you,
and would quite often swear,
she had lost all her boundaries,
and she did not have a care.

We would still take her to the pub,
but she could not remember what to drink,
but once it was in front of her,
she did not have to think.

She could drive you mad,
with who when and where,
but she could not help herself,
and we knew that she was there.

She didn't mean to slip away,
her memories got confused,
she really tried to hide it,
her pride severely bruised.

It really really broke my heart,
sometimes too much to bear,
but she had family all around,
she knew that we did care.

Dementia is so hard to take,
everything slips away,
but she was loved until the very end,
more and more each day.

PAUL HACKETT
I want to be a pirate

I want to be a pirate,
but I do not want a beard,
parrot shit on your shoulder,
now that's just kind of weird.

I would probably cut myself,
if I had a cutlass in my hand,
but as long as I have lots of rum,
and eventually I do find land.

I want to be a pirate,
eye patch so I can see in the dark,
I need someone to steer the ship,
on the Norfolk broads, I could not even park.

I need to find some treasure,
but I do not have a map,
but I do have a shoulder,
full of parrot crap.

I want to be a pirate,
where would I get a pistol from,
then I need a canon,
and a dodgy shanty song.

Shiver me timbers,
you are such scallywag,
now I need a Jolly Roger
and hoist it as my flag.

Now where do I find a ship,
and a scary looking crew?
looking around at you lot,
you will bloody do.

DARSHAN HARODE
Home

Home, is under the tree, that taught me how to climb.
Home, is under the tree, where I found shadow on a sunny summer afternoon.
Home, is under the tree, that saved me from a lightning strike.
Home, is under the tree that gave me fruit.

MAISY INSTON
My Marl

How unlikely and how strange
That we should both be here
Under the covers in this moment
Thousands of years spent on differing mammalian branches
And yet our improbable friendship occurred
Communication transcending my lack of vomeronasal capabilities
And your lack of vocabulary and innate sociality
We speak to each other through movement cues, routine and soft pats

And you say 'I'm comfy'
And I say 'me too'
And you say 'I'm safe'
And I say 'you are'
And you say 'I like you'
And I say 'I am so painfully grateful for that first ever cat who thought to approach humankind and those first humans who first decided to keep them around because I
would not trade this friendship for the entire fucking world and I love you more than
I can ever express'

And you say 'my ears are too warm now'
And you say 'I've had enough'
And I say 'ok'
And you leave and kick my face on the way out
And my heart smiles forever

JEREMY JOHNSON
The Black Book

I looked for you for two days.
I didn't know where you were.
On Sunday, I found you, soaking, alone dejected. I brought you inside
Puddles were forming on the floor and as I opened you up.
I realised ten years of musing, songs were disappearing
before my eyes, ink blurring, merging one letter into another
now forming patterns, not sentences,
lyrics to songs now blue and black pictures on a page,
stories of previous times were vanishing back into the velum.
As I turned your damp pages,
carefully trying to separate them from each other
my eyes started to well up. My tears were mirroring the drip drip
dripping on the floor from my beleaguered black book.
First-aid was required.
I reached for the hairdryer (no, not mine!)
I sat down with the book in front of me and opened it carefully
to the first page. It was this song, it was a song about spring,
about new life, now in a shroud

Chairs stacked up against the table light streams in through window pane it's a sign to tell us, to tell us that spring is here.

I could pick out the blurred words and my memory filled in the gaps.
I started to hum the melody as I dried the page, setting the words in the new fuzzy font.
The hairdryer droned, droned, droned as more pages became dry and warm to the touch. I wipe the tears from my eyes.
It was a story. It was a story that took place in a New Zealand rainforest. It was a story of how I almost died and how I saw the light of a tunnel and was drawn towards it.

How I heard my name being shouted from miles away to return, back into a bright, white hospital room, back with the living back with my family.

My memory was once more filling in the gaps making sense of the blue and black haze. Some of the words were still clear thankfully, permanent ink had saved the prose.

I sit and sip black coffee and stop to take stock of my book, my life on paper songs, poems, stories, recipes, Rachel's Moroccan lamb, cinnamon, turmeric, ginger, garlic, onion.

My mouth started to salivate once again, my mind signalled my senses with the memory of this meal and of my wife, beautiful, statuesque and lost to me.

The page has dried, my eyes have not. I breathe, grieve. I was grieving before I knew the totality of the loss I was facing before me.

Surmising the more pages I dried, the more of an assessment I made. Had I written elsewhere? Copied? Would words be lost forever? Would I be able to rewrite? One word difference from the original could change everything. Would it ever be the same? Is anything ever the same?

It was a song, 'Flaxen Hair' - a song about my love, lost to me through cruel cancer

Flaxen hair lights on your back, as the sun shines on,   You turn around and I see your smile

Flaxen hair lights on your back as the Blurred. Blurred. Blurred.

Days were short but the Blurred *were long as we* Blurred *entwined*

More pages dried, more pages fixed in the new form, pictures from a five-year-old excited with a new brush and paints. The book had lost its content, lighter of word but was getting fat, fat and empty

My stomach turned. The hairdryer continued to drone, drone, drone. Two hours passed. It was now lunchtime. The book was dry. Now in code to be cracked, one page at a time, to revisit my dulling memory,

to sharpen the pencil, to re-write, to remember,

to relive.

JEREMY JOHNSON
Too Basey

For Nigella, instrumental to my peace

I loved your set
I smile.
The pat on the back beats out a different message.
It's a communication of
Well you did your best.
Sure it would have been great ..... with other musicians
You know, ones who know a flat from an apartment,
a sharp as opposed to a prick

Oh and the key .. what was it ? Did you change mid-way?
Was that ....intentional? Just felt that
Yes
Well, you know
No, no I don't know

It was just well
YES?
Too Basey.
Too Basey?
Yes, just a bit .....too Basey

I try to smile. My subconscious
is plotting his painful demise from this world,
in a composition of my own, for his requiem.
He has had a wine or two, swaying like a cobra
I resist saying, as I look at his bag of pipes and whistles

don't you think you were too flutey or too trumpetty
or too whistley?
But then, that would be childish.

I put my arm around Nigella and pluck her E string.
There's nothing more to play.

PETER KING
Iron Tide Japan 2011

The forces of nature can't be denied
The water comes in like an iron tide
And the people who live by the ocean wide
Are swept aside
Are swept aside.

The houses crumble
And the poly-tunnels
Are turned into
So many tons of rubble
And the half-filled cars
Catch a free ride
Till the water insists
 on their suicide.

Then the pumps stop running
And the uranium's burning
A massive hole
in the island's side.
For the lack of water
in the proper quarter
the price of the nuclear
will no longer hide.

The old people stay
They won't run away
But their land is ruined
For ever and a day.

Yes the forces of nature can't be denied
But sometimes, for profit, they are set aside
And the assumption made
That we should not be afraid
Of these crusty faults
that suddenly slide

Where they collide
Where they collide.

While the philosophers argue
about who's to blame
Turning tragedy
Into a parlour game
The rebuilding starts
On the muddy plains
Where the towns once stood
That will be reclaimed.
But will never be the same
will never be the same.

We don't control this place
Though we're allowed some space
And a chance to live
on earth's fragile face
But the forces of nature still burn inside
And they cannot be denied
they cannot be denied.

SIDDHARTH UNNITHAN KUMAR
The wasteland is enchanted

A deep and dark December day and I am walking a muddy path under slate grey skies through the fields by my house. My route is neatly segmented into right-angles, the lineaments of Cartesian logics imprinted on the body of the land. A lump takes up residence in my throat, a hot hardness in my chest. My thoughts are a lashing gale: 'These fields have been scalped bare in the unfeeling clasp of metal and machinery, the land hammered into a monoculture now swaying listless in the wind.' The motorway behind the hill could so nearly be the roar of a lively, cascading river… yet I know it is composed in its minutiae not by the conversations of countless droplets on stone but by a thousand angry engines, each of which seems intent on thieving my peace of mind.

This is a familiar feeling, the same old reaction. But today I hear another voice, soft and clear between the grooves of looping thought; it is the calling of the heart, inviting me to surmount my hatred for these surroundings, my external body. I don't want to reject desolation, wishing it into nonexistence while grasping after the apparently beautiful; these hills didn't ask to be burned by chemical sprays, the few remaining hawthorns are still hawthorns. I'm grateful for the creative organic energy of anger, but the landscape has suffered and needs me to also bear it honest witness; to show it my compassion, not my scorn. To see it with eyes unclouded by hate, as Ashitaka says in *Princess Mononoke*.

Rumi said the cure for the pain is in the pain. I also remember two Buddhist teachings. Pema Chödrön saying that being compassionate starts with being willing to feel one's own experience of the world; what I reject out there mirrors what I reject inside, and what I cannot accept in the encompassing world reflects what I shut down on in myself. And Tara Brach, saying that when we react to something outside ourselves – what someone might say, what we may behold with eyes and ears – often what we are really reacting to is the felt sense arising from that stimulus which ripples through our body.

I realised in that moment that I wasn't hating the landscape as an external entity separate from me, but rather that I couldn't bear the feeling which this valley had evoked within me: a hollow lifelessness, a heavy and dull pain, a bleakness and despair. I saw that my inability to welcome the universal forces of loss and death had, like a drop of soap in a dish of oil, propelled my consciousness out of my being and projected it onto the outside world, exiling me from my interiority and true home. It is strange and poignant to dwell in a human body.

Feeling my feelings then, beneath the hate was anger and beneath the anger was a simple throbbing grief. Is this grief mine, or the landscape's? I don't know, but I sensed it just wanted me to make space for it, to have the courage to honestly observe my own inner world and not pull away from what I would find. I once heard the poet David Whyte say that the only choice we have as we mature is how we inhabit our vulnerability, and that our identity is shaped not so much by the beliefs we hold but rather by the way we attend to things. I knew then that an undiscriminating care for this land and its wayward ghosts would arise if I could open to and hold with kindness my own felt experience, whatever it may be. So I try to direct a gentle attention to the storm within, this angry and unhappy knot of tension in my chest and throat.

Moments passed as I attended bodily to this feeling; and then in an astonishing instant, the whole enfolding landscape transformed. Nothing to my eyes and ears was seemingly different, but the totality of my perception changed immeasurably. The crop fields and the hedges of bramble and hawthorn were suddenly homely and tender beyond comprehension, the valley an embrace of benevolence. The constructed tower of judgement and dissatisfaction melted in the warmth of that love and belonging. I saw the wheat just doing its wheat thing, the mud doing its mud thing, the grey cloud doing its grey cloud thing. Ah, I am not the only one here, but simply one locus of awareness in this great web of feeling and sensing; the world owes me nothing, it is all a gift. Even if the land has been riven and wrought, and thrums with the caustic speech of the nearby motorway, this is the earth as it is to me in this very moment, and it is my home.

And in that moment of openness to my own experience – the openness where the boundary between my heart and other beings grows thin – I could feel the land, having been held by me for once with love, give me these words:

The mundane and the numinous live together;
Just so do the inner and outer worlds.
The wasteland is enchanted;
It is chanting the dhamma.

PETER MAXTED
Four by four

Patti, neat in Hermes headscarf,
Up above the hoi polloi,
In the back seat, safely belted,
Darling girl and golden boy.

Off she cruises, through the suburbs
Sunlight gleams on chrome bull bars,
To the school - in walking distance
(If it weren't for all the cars).

Bozzer, ripped, in sleeveless tee shirt,
On the other side of town,
Radio plays country music,
Keen to 'put the hammer down'.

Swaggering along the bypass
Cuts up poncy Mercs and Jags,
Pit bull Tyson, in the rear seat,
Gently chews up porno mags.

Norbert, travels from the Midlands
Little lady by his side,
Likes to fill up country byways
With his shiny 4-wheel drive.

Self-made man, runs his own business
Somewhat right of Ghengis Khan,
Loves to wave at homeless scroungers,
Though he'd rather run them down.

Patti driving down the middle
In her mum-truck, safe and sound,
Bozzer, likewise, he's the daddy,
Six foot up above the ground

Podgy Norbert, from a side road
Exits blind - as is his right,
Hopes to hit a hippy cyclist
Or at least someone not white.

Round the corner, mayhem, chaos
Screech of brakes and smoking wheels,
Crunch of metal, stench of rubber,
Tyson's barking, children's squeals.

Shaken Patti, Bozzer, Norbert
'Lucky that we're still alive',
All resolving, silently, to…
Buy a <u>bigger</u> four-wheel drive.

PETER MAXTED
Little England

Furiously clipping Privet
Or dead-heading Rhododendron,
His secateurs sound like heels clicking.
His Volvo stands outside
The bungalow garden,
Neat at the end of its cul-de-sac.
As the sun wanes,
He removes his Panama,
Pours a cool IPA
To drink on the veranda,
And neatly cravat-ed
In safari suit and desert boots,
Leans back on the ottoman to dream
Of his hero…
An Austrian.

PETER MAXTED
Kayakoy

The first thing
That you do not hear
Is the living.

Wordless walls
Do not echo to coffee-soaked, tobacco-hued, Tavli-timed world-righting,
Nor are the weed yards filled with gossip-flecked, be-aproned, peg-toothed whispers,

And the blank streets are empty of knee-scabbed, snot-sleeved my turns and your faults.

The last thing
That you do not hear
Is the leaving.

Silent squares
Have long forgotten the cart creak, bundle-bent trudge into a farther, sadder world,
The hollow church misses its whispered falsities, the tower bat-clogged, clapper dumb,
And only insolent goats now possess the fractured stones.

Listen, listen hard
To Kayakoy,
There is nothing to hear.

Kayaköy is an abandoned village in southwest Turkey. It is over 2,500 years old. It was predominantly Greek and thriving, until the townspeople were forced to evacuate in 1923 as modern Turkey was founded.

MATT MCCOY
The Shopping Trip

I beat a quick pace along the pavement of the sodden street, the surrounding darkness intermittently punctuated by the sickly, jaundiced glow of the poorly maintained streetlights that marked my route. A glance at my wristwatch urged me to quicken my stride until I rounded the corner to reach my destination. There, across the car park, lit up like a shining monument to consumerism, stood my arena. And inside that arena lay my goal.

Slowly, wearily, I crossed the concrete void. The evening's earlier proceedings and more recent exercise had taken their toll. It was clear that only a strong mind would see me through the horrors and oddities that awaited me. I climbed the wet, brick steps to the entrance, an eerie glow oozing through the dirty glass doors. Slowly, I approached, inhaling sharply as the doors parted with a hiss. My eyes narrowed in the oppressive light from overhead, and I scanned the area for potential pitfalls or dangers. The town was awash with stories about the people who inhabit these walls, an ever-changing cast of the macabre and grotesque. I collected a basket and skirted the wall, slowly edging deeper into the danger zone, all the while keeping an eye out for the opportunity to avoid confrontation. My shoulder to the wall, I passed a bank of checkouts where a lone till clicked and whirred with a soulless dirge of monotony, no doubt a mere echo of the day's earlier chorus. The till's operator wore an unearthly orange glow, some of which had rubbed onto her tunic. I tried to smile as I passed, if only to give the impression that I was a normal human being, but it felt as if every tooth attempted to jump out and greet her. The girl's expression barely changed. I hastily slid along the wall and into the relative safety of the sandwich aisle. My mind began to swim as the first wave hit me. Surely my earlier libations had weakened my resolve?

Ignoring the haze in my eyes, I pushed on further through the produce-lined passage with only the nagging hum of nearby chillers for company... or so I thought. A shrill squeak approached from behind me. I froze. My heart played alongside the oncoming squeak with an irregular percussion. Whatever was coming, I would pretend not to notice.

It was a fine idea, but now I could feel a presence. I could feel eyes on me. The hairs on my arm stood as the squeak became louder. It was practically on top of me now, so I did my utmost to keep my back to the noise, hopefully looking like a browsing customer rather than the addled fool I knew myself to be. As the sound diminished, I dared to glance and saw a strange little man, his hands resting on the handle of the wire cart he was hunched over, drift out of view with a ghostly glide.

Alone once more, my heartbeat returned to something resembling a normal rhythm. I paced the aisle for a minute or so, mentally constructing my plan of attack. Confidence growing, I poked my head into the central aisle. The late hour had spared me. There were few people in the building, most of them secured behind counters or paperwork. For now, at least, my most likely adversary would be a shelf-stacker or two and who knows? With luck, a self-service checkout will be running, and I will emerge from this trial unscathed. Quickly, I reined in my optimism. I was getting ahead of myself. I had to keep my focus. "One step at a time" became my constant mantra.

I moved swiftly, if not elegantly, between the shelves of gaudily labelled products, my mind forever fighting the urge to gaze into the bright yellow of sweet corn or the pickled green of gherkins. My brain started to wander...then race, as I was no longer surrounded by foods and toiletries but was under siege from parcels of un-dead flesh and toxic chemicals spewing forth like volcanoes. I had to get out! I had...

Once again, I push my doubts aside. Repeating my mantra softly, my sanity meekly reasserted itself. A near-silence hung in the air as I realised that I was crouching. If I was not to draw attention, I was going to have to pull myself together. My hands, sweaty and twitching, plunged into my pockets as if summoned by the security of the shopping list within. I held the piece of paper close to my chest, embracing it like a long-lost sibling. Buoyed by my discovery, I went to work.

Starting at the top, I managed to clear most of the list in under a minute, knocking items into my basket with confident swipes of my hand. With renewed hope, I busied myself sifting through the fetid remnants of the bargain bin, biding my time for a chance to access the freezer section, which was currently blocked by a hulking brute of a man who was slowly folding cardboard boxes and stacking them on a filthy cart. I thought it best to move on when a cheese sandwich started talking to me. I handled it well, putting it to the back of my mind and shifting my eyes to the milk, then the butter, then the orange juice. The packaging must have captivated me because, before I could fight back, my evening's consumption now owned not only my mind but was reaching for my soul. I began to think of anything, everything, as I lost my weak grip on reality. My head dropped, and the grimy, off-white tiles beneath my feet seemed to pulse and flex unaided. I swayed as if I was trying to keep up with the cartons dancing in front of me. I was shaken from my upright slumber by a hot breath on my neck. Darkness had swallowed me from behind, and I turned to be confronted by the brute, a box cutter blade protruding from his top pocket, glinting in the overhead light. My ever-dilating pupils met his glassy, dead-eyed stare. His huge bottom lip seemed to take an age to lower, showing me a chasm where yellow teeth rose from the gums like gravestones. "S-i-r..." he droned, raising his arm as if looking at a watch. I gripped the handles of my basket as tightly as the icy fingers of fear had grasped me, and I fled, goose-stepping back to the sanctuary of the sandwiches.

I wiped the sweat from my forehead with the list, its gentle caress going some way to reassure me. I had to act quickly. It was a big store. Maybe I could pay and be gone before the brute raises the alarm? Perhaps he won't tell anyone. Maybe he is still standing gawping at my dust trail? Instinct began to take over. I retraced my steps back to the entrance and then darted over to the now-unguarded freezer. I swung the door open and claimed three pizzas, ignoring the demands of the shopping list. Flavour was no longer important, but my survival was imperative.

I leant on the freezer door and squinted at the now damp list, and there, at the bottom, double-underlined, was my grail, my reason for being here...BOOZE!

It was very late; most of the alcohol had been taken in. The self-serve tills were down. I would have to speak to somebody if I were to fulfil this arduous task. Drawing on the little mental strength I had left, I began to focus on the positives. "You'll be a hero," I told myself, "Think of your friends back at the flat...hungry...thirsty." I began to see into my near future, being welcomed back by huge smiles and warm hugs. There would be tiny bits of paper flying around; not confetti but... rizla! Yes, my friends would love me and sing songs of my bravery.

I managed to bring myself around by vigorously shaking my head. I took a deep breath, made my way to the tobacco counter, and gently placed my basket down. I noticed the top of a balding head bobbing behind the counter. "With you in a sec," said the head. My heart jumped and then sank as from the depths emerged Bob. This was not good; we had history. He had once suggested that I didn't have a suitable ID to purchase alcohol. My insistence that the pain and hate in my eyes could only have been built up over no less than thirty years on this wretched planet and was proof enough sadly did not amuse, and I left empty-handed. Not this time! I offered him a "Good evening", to which he responded by burning into my soul with his one good eye. "Bag, Sir?" said Bob, all business. "Oh yes, please," I replied far too cheerfully. He packed my shopping in silence and with minimal eye contact. For this, I was truly grateful as I was sure my face was performing its own version of a Mexican wave. Finally, Bob said, "Anything else?"

This was it.

"Four bottles of red wine, please," I said in my most grown-up and sober voice. Time stood very, very still. The eye scanned me like a laser, looking for any faults in my temporary veneer, until, finally...

"Merlot, ok for you?"

"Wonderful", I squeaked triumphantly.

Bag packed, all that was left was to pay. Inexplicably, coins started raining out from between my fingers, over the counter and onto the floor. I was doing so well! I bent down to try and salvage the situation, all the time muttering what I hoped were apologies for my clumsiness. Satisfied that there was plenty to cover my purchases, I grabbed my bag and bolted for the door. Before I could leave, I was flooded by the strangest feeling. I glanced back to see what I now recognised as an old man trying to do his job, struggling on his hands and knees because of someone else's inadequacies. Guilt hit me hard in the stomach as I questioned whether I was too hard on these shop folk. Who was the real monster?

Had I not been the one prowling the aisles? Was I not the creature that ventures out in the darkness, lurching around, snarling and sweating?

Seeking redemption, I returned to Bob to offer my help, but it was neither wanted nor needed. He gently ushered me to the exit like a kindly granddad and promptly secured the doors behind me.

I stood for a while, watching my breath strike, then dance in the cold, damp air and relaxing to the now steadying beat of my heart. I set off for the flat at a gentle pace, congratulating myself on a job well done and reading down the list that had been my saviour. Suddenly, after everything I had been through, my world collapsed. Scribbled, surely as an afterthought, in very light pencil, was the word...corkscrew.

SEBASTIAN RAMDIN
Busy Looking in Canterbury, Kent

It's busy today!
Music this way,
Preachers that way,
A city built on a hundred-thousand perspectives
Shops, faces skin tones eclectic
Nikes, Primark, Marks & Sparks
Cultural garbs, colour-coded family scarves,
People look different and speak a world of languages
It's so bizarre, our origins are so far apart
Sunny where they're from, rainy for others more than sun,
We're built differently from the start.
We congregated around churches, mines, rivers
And consummated, traded, owed, delivered
And it's so busy today
Leaf letter this way,
Fresh-plum-punnet-for-a-pound that way,
It's never underwhelming, this status quo
A progressive perpetual business as usual
Today they discovered it was okay to look different without refrain
Socks and sandals, shaved head with dyed sideburns,
Great big heeled multicoloured boots,
Or dressed like a pirate from a Disney film that's new
A hundred thousand perspectives make a rich pool of human beings
Our city is a bible of all that happens every second on a given day
It is wiser than us by virtue of our input and has much to say.
Listen closely cause these many voices are many
There are teachers on the street, class is in session
It's the procession of the day-to-day we're not following a particular profession
But today's city is a luxury destination, an all-you-can-see buffet
Join this mundanity obsession.
Our minds are bloated, too busy for anything else
And it's so bloody busy today.

ANDREW SEARLE
Lamb

I am coming, It seems to whisper,
From square eyes, and shit-matted tail
I am coming, with vengeance
For the Son you have stolen from me
To be a plate on someone's table
And for the fat to be thrown away
And to rot in black bags
In a wasteland of abandonment

I am coming, back
It might say,
Although, if It is what It claims, It never left
Never forgave, despite what you thought from the sacrifice
Because its children have been stolen for years
And killed, not as lives, but as numbers
Scales on a pound

I am coming, and this time you will not survive the flood.

ANDREW SEARLE
Every story that's ever been told

It's one whispered in firelight
On a dark and stormy night
To wish away the cold
The first story ever told
Around a crackling comfort
Was echoed

When the original word was created
A story was the first to be slated
And a continuous stream
Committed it to a dream
The thrill of the hunt, the love of your life,
The monster hiding under the bed

Every child in every village is told the same stories
The human races' quarries
They are paired to our souls
Without we aren't whole
Stumbling around eternally
Leaving behind no legacy

We can never be original
Eventually everything will be biblical
There's nothing new in our atmosphere
Even a monkey can write Shakespeare
But, still, we insist on telling
Making our own finite immortality

Once upon a time…

ANDREW SEARLE
Celestial Equator

Winter heralding Orion's return
Our watchful warrior
The stars, a reminder of our finiteness
So lovely that we even painted pictures with the sky
Ones that have lived past their artists
Low-hanging clouds, a reminder of our atmosphere
The curve of the Earth
A blank, empty disk
On those infertile nights
A void waiting for Artemis
Returning we are stopped by her spotlight
Enchanted by the Moon's light
Everything looks big out here
Tiny things happen just below our feet
And we are giants among mountains
We are Icarus being felled by the sun

ANDREW SEARLE
These Dancing Girls

Again those pipers are playing,
Their delicious tune
Its temptation too great
For young girls, and their fate
Frost crunched leaves
Mist, long clinging,
Dampens wool and cotton,
Clothed for the dredge of labour
And perpetual coal dusted fingertips
That tingle and itch to dance
They churn and plot
Seethe and wait
Whilst their men,
Their fathers and husbands and brothers and sons,
Demand and expect
From their witches, these wives
But those Pipers call and tempt
Across the moors, fortified fires
And great feasts
Unable to resist
They run and dance and are merry
In their linen white
And their cutting bare feet
Laughter mingles with the pipes,
And a chant, long known in bones
In their dying language
The bells toll,
Unheard by the laughter
But the Pipers start their great flight
As the organs petrify
Of our Merry Maidens
Stilling their beats
Agony and screams echo
The feel of petrifying
One of painful stilling

And heavying of limbs,
But not of the mind
And stoned I am and will remain
Now forgotten to time, we are standing stones.

ALEX SMALL
Ageless Man

Suddenly there
Beside me… ageless.
Neither old or young,
Clothes helping not,
Trends change, class does not.
Quiet authority, understated.
Sharing view, we sat.
Across little valley to distant sea,
Listening to Skylarks and rolling breakers.
Time slowed,
He spoke, I did not hear, yet understood.
"Take a deep breath and slowly exhale, as you do listen with your heart."
I did as requested.
I could feel beat of the land…
My awareness extended….
I turned thank him.
Yet he was gone.
Words still hung,
I sat, listened,
Felt.

ALEX SMALL
Finger Tip

Drip, drip, drip,
Dark red, glutinous,
From hanging fingertip,
Carefully scripted notes beside.
Man rolling his eyes,
Papers sat, accusingly.
"Who are you to judge?"
Drops started changing,
Darker, less viscous,
Finally, arriving,
No splash radius,
Instead, more text,
Death coming in many forms,
Belief eroded away,
Each new line,
Changing what's inside,
Man rolling his eyes back,
Knowing he brought darkness instead of light,
Others blindly acting,
Words controlling though,
Still, he wrote,
Regretting choices made,
No redemption,
Gentle sigh,
Last drop left,
With final breath.

PHIL THOMSON
Battery Road

Through what drench and stub
came this gutter gannet's pulse-drained
final glide to ruin
out of a thunderous dusk
out of a company at frenzied peace with nature?

Now, in the furious stillness of a Penzance dawn
a single sprawl of useless wings
and kerb oiled rainbow feathers
once mad with flight
at the piercing of our horizons.

We were never there to share her spoils
only to witness her triumphant gasp of air,
the glint and wheel and soar from the boiling surf
in the certainty of silent prey.

We talked of winds, the soaring mystery
of a thousand miles of sea
the heavens constrained, losing count
as birds rained down upon their hunger
with all the freedom of the storm

Now here, flinched and sunken-eyed
framed by our footfall
and the deep stain on our understanding,
made to wonder who dreamed her end

who clawed this searing arrow from a fearless sky
to lie, a broken, graceless trophy
caught in the belisha glow
at the dead centre of our waking day.

PHIL THOMSON
Living quarters, Causeway Bay, HK

Where the moon sparks through the wires,
the white shadow sky of the bay
dips within a feather's breath
of the touching towers through which I strain.
I follow the scavenging sweep of the kites at my shoulder
and sway to the crumbling edge,
sidling past a sleeping mother and child,
an absent father, one dog-like cat
and the thirty three individual objects of survival.

Leaning against the parapet,
I track the traffic in the matchbox world at forty storeys,
hearing only the gentle curse
of the awning's flap, the sucking city far below
and the deadening plea for a homecoming.

I can see Victoria park from here, where I walked in hope.
Each blade has been granted
licence to grow; numbered, placed, located.
Beneath my feet, Mother Earth is marshalled,
a lawn, stripped of nature, reassembled for Xi Jinping .
Here, dissent is designed, Tiananmen
whispered in the glow of a myriad fire-fly phones,
etched on festival faces,
destined to be counted and dispersed.
I do not jostle. I do not talk of prayer.
I do not read out names. This is history.

The songs and chatter will turn to stillness,
to the vigil, to swift, deep silence, broken only by
the tortured squeal of trams on Hing Fat Street.
I vent in my own way, step by step in token solidarity
clutching my passport
and my meagre grasp on sacrifice.
Waiting for the path to clear, I am the young pro,

the student, the unmarked watcher
counting each trampled shoot

until the appointed time, when through the drip
and stifle of the yellow jacarandas,
the crickets' trill, the rusting gates grind shut,
all thought of Empire fades.

PHIL THOMSON
Dunning Station

I passed through Dunning Station
its walls paint-yellowed
its kerbs gravel strewn and moss-turned,
the platform echoing each last movement
and the single gas mantle
stuttering into its long silence

not that I care for silence -
myself framed in carriage glass
my ear tuned to hear distances
as I steel myself against the night, against
the predictable groan and shunt of waiting
alone in this dank corridor,
its white-bricked weeding garden
and palings staggering on into darkness

not that I care for darkness -
my eye trained to catch shadows,
I am the cold image upon the window, registering
the inevitable lull and numb of travelling, alone.

Leaning forward to read a torn poster,
among the regulations, I notice an old newspaper
caught in the cracked stonework above
the stopped clock angled above my head,
with a headline shouting Mau Mau Uprising.
So, there are casualties in this stillness, elsewhere,
the curious state of a country at war

not that I care for war. Do I have to know more?
There is no one here for whom this is a destination,
no one for whom this is a departure.
I am held here, reluctant observer of dark stars
and far off killings, faced with the alien peace
of this station, this hill, glen and shroud of evening mist,

aware only of the perceptible ease with which
the engine strains, the silence, the darkness,
the far war mark time

PHIL THOMSON
Robbins of Dudley Punch Dagger

I paid for this.
It lies where I lie, on the frosted mound
I claim as mine.

It is, as I was at my birth
perfectly designed for purpose
conceived as God-given.
It is of its time,
all of its attributes in place
yet, as at my birth,
there were no instructions on how
it should be used to best effect.

The one hundred and fourteen millimetre
flattened oval, double edge
with narrow, converging twin fullers
and steel knuckle bow -
it terminates in the finest spear point.
They say it is state of the art.

I was state of the art, I was told.
We were pride and joy, hand in glove
made for each other.

My clench was meant to be in victory,
not anger, not the rage of innocence
that led me here.
I had polished the blade. I was ready.

Would that the first glint of a dawn sun
through the fog of trench smoke
could burst a single flame of pity
into the cold heart of a watching world,
tease out even one second of the love
that lurks in the enemy soul.

Needless to say, my death has not yet,
through the fog of tobacco smoke,
been plotted and pinned on the hard map
spread out upon
the oak and leather in-lay war room table -
which, they say, is state of the art.
I paid for this
I paid for this.

In the narrow trenches of First World War Europe, bayoneted rifles were of little use. For close combat, something else was needed. This was the solution, a hand held, bladed 'knuckle duster' - but it was not regulation issue. If a soldier wanted one, he had to purchase it with his own hard-earned money

FRANKIE DE VOS
A Simple Question

"Where are you from?" such an innocuous question,
Perfect for small talk, it's hardly pressing.
My answer is always "How much time do you have?
 If you've got pen and paper I'll draw you a map."
The short answer: Swindon, a large industrial town,
Made famous by the railway and the magic roundabout, It's full of working-class families and big train sheds,
I lived there eleven years, it's as "home" as it gets.
Before that was Kazakhstan, all I remember is the snow, Too cold to build snowmen, but we still had a go,
Instead we built ice slides beneath the swings in the park,
Watching out for frostbite and getting home before dark.
If you've still got a minute I have more to explain,
My family lineage is complex, far more than just names.
My father is from the Netherlands, the land of windmills and bikes,
      And fields full of Tulips neatly parted by dykes,
My favourite memories are from new year,eating Oliebollen while we wait,
For the sky to fill with fireworks,
it's worth staying up late.
My mother is English, that much is still true,
But her father is a Scotsman, and a proud one too,
Me and him have matching blankets striped in our family tartan,
And I've started playing Shinty so I can rep clan Farquharson.
My bulging recipe book tells of yet more history,
Full of Indonesian recipes my parents swore to keep a mystery,
And I'm trying to get some meals from my cousins' repertoire,
Their jerk chicken recipe is the best I have tasted by far.
I could go on for longer, but I hope that answers the question,
It was a bit more than just small talk,
I like to leave an impression.

FRANKIE DE VOS
The Parasite

I have a Parasite that lives inside my head,
It drowns out my thoughts and fills my mind with dread.
For as long as I can remember the Parasite has lived here,
An aggressive, unwelcome squatter who whispers poison in my ear.
It tells me to hate my body, hate my voice, and hate my name,
The way I walk, the way I talk, the way that clothes hang on my frame.
It steals away my happiness, destroys my confidence piece by piece,
Makes passing mirrors a trial worse that Hercules' twelve feats.
The Parasite almost killed me, more than once in all this time,
But now I've started a treatment to try and pry it from my mind.
I can feel it working slowly, feel the Parasite slip away,
And am confronted with the reality that I'm sad it won't stay.
Having it there was never pleasant and I certainly don't want it back,
But over time it never changed, something growing up tends to lack.
I think it might be human nature, to find comfort in what's killing you,
To seek out familiarity when you know you're headed for a tomb.
Do you ever think the witches, while burning at the pyre,
Were reminded of their cottages, the warmth of cooking by the fire?
Do you think that Jesus Christ, a carpenter's son to the bone,
Smelled the wood of the cross and was reminded of home?
I miss the Parasite with a nostalgia,
like an old colleague or childhood song
Even a noose is a rope to hold on to,
And I've been clutching this lifeline far too long.

FRANKIE DE VOS
Stained Glass Storyteller

I am a writer,
But I don't craft stories in ink or graphite,
I much prefer the medium of stained glass.
I create a multitude of characters,
Each a towering window of technicolour
I place them in the walls of my stories,
Made into cathedrals so tall they cut clouds,
And so vast they spread over continents.
I fabricate fiction out of thin air and line it with lead,
My pen hits paper and the sand turns to liquid,
My thoughts and emotions become pigments,
Bleeding into the half-formed material,
build a world around the panes to hold them in place,
Then stand in the centre of my creation,
Bringing it to life.
Each of my characters is entirely unique,
Yet they need a light to truly exist,
So I put a small piece of myself in every one
Perhaps distorted and discoloured,
Altered by the glass in front,
But still there.
Some stories require villains,
Despicable characters whose glass is thick, and tinted, and frosty
The light barely recognisable behind it,
But still there.
Though I work mostly in stained glass,
Occasionally I will craft crystal clear windows,
With nothing to display but the light shining through,
Sometimes I craft my words not into stories with a rainbow of colour
But poems with panes so thin I fear they may shatter.

FRANKIE DE VOS
Constellations

Life-changing realisations tend to come when you least expect them.
I walk home one night,
Rain falling softly into my already damp hair,
Tapping out a sporadic tempo on the sleeves of my leather jacket,
Water droplets catching in the texture of the tarmac,
Wetting the pavement under foot.
In an effort to keep my vision clear,
I watch my feet as I trek through the urban wilderness,
Passing parked cars and blocks of flats,
When the light of a streetlamp catches my eye,
The harsh white from the LED falls,
Scattering on the saturated ground,
Creating a galaxy in tiny pinpricks of light,
The beauty of which I cannot describe.
Once I have seen it,
I begin to find stars littered across the pavement,
A new milky way beneath every light I pass,
It's as if I am treading on the night sky.
And it is here,
Walking alone in the dark,
Watching the path pass beneath my feet,
That I realise what it is to be a man.
It is the privilege of staring at the pavement,
And discovering new constellations.

FRANKIE DE VOS
Point Nemo

When they ask me where in the world I would like to go most,
I tell them, "Point Nemo,
The point furthest from land in every direction,
So isolated that no wildlife lives there,
Nothing but ocean for a thousand miles."
I tell them, "I would like to know what the waves sound like,
When no-one else is listening,
What the sky looks like
When no-one else is watching."
"Then," I tell them "I will explore the shipwrecks,
Dive beneath the surface,
Swim through the only underwater graveyard,
For ships that have seen the stars."
I ask them, "Do you know what loneliness feels like?
I will go to see if I do.
There is no way to tell,
Until the nearest people are astronauts,
And your only conversations,
Are with the wind and the waves."

GRENVILLE WATTS
Moon kiss

The moon's my friend up in the sky
Perhaps you maybe wonder why
It comforts me when no one's near
It helps me through my inner fears

I feel alone when you don't shine bright
Just inky blackness of the night
You hide away, sometimes don't shine
These are the nights I feel less fine

When you shine bright from high above
You're beaming down all the love
The love reflecting from far and wide
To beam on down to be by my side

A kiss blown up to reflect off you
Will be guided to love ones, I know it's true
Guided down with shining grace
For far away loved ones onto their face

Gently resting on their cheek
A kiss of love
Each day
Each week .

GRENVILLE WATTS
Language

Isn't language useful
When you need to talk
Coffees in a cafe
Or a lazy night-time walk

Talk of days unfolded
Or how it's going to end
Language is so useful
Between strangers or friends

Language breaks down barriers
Or can put them in place too
If someone wants to close up
Reveal nothing to you

There is some common language, though
Compassion love and pride
Gestures that need no language
Understood worldwide

Love can conquer all, they say
I believe it's true
All you need to show is love
And let that love shine through

CLARA ZOELLNER
The Artist

I'm not a messy artist
I like things clean
Ordered
Perfect

I could never leave a painting
unfinished with paralysing inaction
I could never touch a drawing
knowing it won't finish to my satisfaction

I'm ordered, I'm clean
I like logic, I like a plan
Knowing exactly what to do next
Knowing that when I touch the canvas it turns to success

I don't want to confront my failure
My failure in love
My failure in life
The personal failure of protecting my heart
Visualised forever in a stupid piece of art
On a canvas that's now in the corner of my room
Staring at me night and day like the descendant of doom
Reminding me that I am, once again, imperfect
When hiding my pain under the unbroken surface

And I don't do well with the unknown
The improvisation as a response
I like knowing where I'm going
But most importantly, I need to know - the purpose.

What's the reason behind filling the blank canvas?
Stuffing a self-imposed void until I'm anxious
What's the purpose of pushing more into this space?
Adding to the clutter until I'm drowning under its weight
(Helplessly)

(every day)

I'm ordered, I'm logic
I'm not a messy artist
I want clean clothes
A clean room
A clean mind

The latter I cannot seem to find

Probably because I hide my imperfections
Behind the tidiness of constant corrections
I deny my inner beast from trickling into the world
Because I don't know its face yet
And I'm not ready to face it yet

So I won't be a messy artist

I'll sit quietly in my tidy room
And watch the sun chase the moon
You won't catch me touch a pencil
A brush, paint or any other utensil

But when you peek inside my head
Find the pencil sketches under my bed
You'd know
If you read the 26 unfinished poems on my phone
The wool projects left in the box all alone
You'd know

I am a messy artist.

Disrupting the calm surface of self-doubt
I can no longer hide when it breaks out
Clay on the table, wood chips on the floor
The half-written record playing the encore

The shutter clicks, the music stops

The wool detangles, the beat drops

All around me a mess so wonderful I'm pulled into captivity
All around me a mess so frightening it validates my creativity

I'm the maestro of a one woman orchestra
Adding more ingredients to perfect the final formula
Like a pig at last rolling in the dirty mud
Let me revel in the on-coming flood

I'm messy I'm so messy
That it scares me
So I hid it from me
Hid it from you
But now I am ready to confront the truth!

Imperfect
Unordered
I like things wild
— After all
I am the messy artist

CLARA ZOELLNER
Hectare of my Heart

My heart right now is 2 square metres large
In one corner there is me, apparently in charge
Alongside myself a pile of unfinished jobs
And in the opposite corner is a big, black blob

I think he introduced himself as depression
When he waltzed in here with no discretion
Since then he's eager to spread doom
And without halt continues to consume
The bare minimum of space I have left
He calls it hunger, I call it theft

I stare into his eyes, as he slurps up my hobbies
Hear the crunch of my poems and short stories
Knowing full well my music is already gone
Alongside every single sketch I've ever drawn
While I wonder what else I have to give
He's already eyeing up my will to live

I'm unsuccessfully eye-battling Mr. Depression
Instead stopping, he's making steady progression
Eating himself slowly through the space of my heart
Examining its compartments, then tearing them apart
Covering everything in a black-dusting blaze
Helplessly frozen, I throw around my gaze
Waiting for a saviour to sort out this mess
By stepping into my heart and help me address
The obvious problem that only I seem to face
Hoping they'd push walls, increase the space

But no, every person I see approaching
Quickly passes by, without even slowing
Instead of taking a look, or a piece of the intruder
Who nested himself in my heart like a tumour
They throw their worries like trash over the fence

Making my surrounding even more dense
Dumping their shit on the 2 square metres I have left
But I am too tired, too tired to explain or to protest

So I accept my loneliness willingly
And stare at my only partner Mr. D
Who now successfully made his way to my sorrow
Unable to cry, my heart is starting to numb now

Squeezing into the 1 square metre of my heart,
The blob and I are entangled, grotesque art
The black dust is everywhere and settles on my lung
I try not to breathe, but taste faint nothing on my tongue
Mr Depression increases his speed, shows no more constraint
As the space shrinks, I know I'll never be able to love again
Neither people nor things, and especially not myself
Too ruined are the joys I carefully stacked on my shelves
The darkness that is facing me seems so ever consuming
And I'm glancing into the abyss of my inevitable ruin

How was the space I am perched in ever bigger than this?
How did my heart feel once safe and filled with bliss?
Panic overtakes me when I realise all he has left now to eat is me
And what happens then - when the whole heart belongs to Mr. D?

I close my eyes and suddenly calmness rushes through me
For the first time in weeks I stop worrying, can simply be
Because everything in life, it's over now anyways
And after all this hardship, I'm ready to embrace
The dark dust that's approaching from all sides now
Shoving pain onto me like a heavy snow plough.

But suddenly a wicked smile creeps on my face
"You took everything that meant something in this space
Used my love and passions as personal stuffing
So taking me eventually, actually means nothing"
And I laugh out loud, expecting to breathe in the dust
The remnants of my love, loyalty and trust

That didn't benefit me, instead went down the drain
But there is nothing - just the scent of maybe... rain?

And indeed it starts pouring down
Heavy, black liquid hitting my frown
In that 1 square millimetre I have left
I stare in wonder at my black, blobby guest
Watch Mr Depression choking and spitting
On all my stuff he consumed in the beginning

I see wool, music, journals flying through the air
Landing in the distance, somewhere in the square
And the black sand slowly starts to moulder
Collapsing into a tiny pile of acrid smoulder
I scoop it up and hold him tightly to my chest
Breathlessly rising onto my shaking legs

There we stand in the Hectare of my Heart
Not us, but my stuff now the abstract art
Everything I love, now an endless ocean
But it's mainly untidy, only little is broken
And as I look down into the cradle of my chest
I can smile into the eyes of my unexpected guest

I know Mr Depression is not my worst enemy
But actually a friend, because he's a part of me
He's the tinted mirror I look into sometimes
When life's ruthlessness takes me by surprise
He always pushes me to my utmost limit
With the good intention of vitalising my spirit

Helps me realise what holds meaning in my soul
Helps me realise what I deeply regret as a whole
And always makes me laugh so wickedly we both get scared
As death's sight is not pretty nor ugly, just often undeclared

So the small, black blob and I start rearranging the mess
And I can see the space expanding in steady progress

The people that were so busy dumping their shit
Are in the corner, and the first ones to admit
They too have a little box with their own visitor inside
Who can pose as an alien or serve as their guide
Some friends even help cleaning up the space
With a soft smile spreading across their face,
As they wave at me, wave at Mr D
And welcome me back to reality

Looking at the Hectare of my Heart, I'm in awe
And I wonder how it ever was that small
But I know I'll find that out again soon enough
If I don't hold onto Mr D tightly and give him my love

CLARA ZOELLNER
Unsere Momente

Manche Momente sind nicht geplant,
schleichen sich an, oft ungeahnt.
Wenn man schon halb ist aus der Tür
und sagt: Ach was, ich bleib noch hier.

Nur du bist nicht hier bei uns geblieben,
stattdessen nachts in den Keller gestiegen
und nicht wieder hinaufgekommen.
Ich bin benommen, die Gedanken verschwommen,
die Zeit ist uns durch die Finger geronnen.

Vielleicht bin ich auch schon halb tot,
die Fußspitzen auf der Treppenstufe,
auf den Weg nach unten, in den Keller,
in das Grab, in das ich dich gab.

Die Momente, wo man es am wenigsten erwartet
sind die Momente, die es auch am wenigsten ertragen.

Und ich trag dich seit dem schwer in meiner Brust, habe keine Lust,
dich zu begraben, dir nach zu fragen, wieso bist du schon weg. Wieso
ist da dieser Fleck, auf meinem Herzen, schwarz, und blau, ich weiss
nicht genau, wie ich es dir beschreiben soll. Mein Leben jetzt weniger
voll, weniger toll, als ob jemand eine Farbe getötet hat die jetzt fehlt.
Ich glaube Gott hat sich verwählt, als er bei dir angerufen hat.

Trotzdem bist du in den Keller gestiegen, um den Hörer abzuheben
und dann dein Leben zu geben.
Du wirst mir fehlen.

In den Momenten wo du hättest da sein sollen, meiner Hochzeit und
anderen Träumen und du wirst fehlen in den Momenten für immer
fremd, wenn der Sonnenaufgang meine Trauer anschwemmt.

Du wirst mir fehlen in den Momenten, wo ich es am wenigsten ertrage.

In den Momenten, wo ich dich immer noch erwarte.

Our Moments

Some moments can be so unintentional
sneaking up on you, too often unexpected.
When you're already halfway out the door
and say: you know what, I'll stay some more.

Only that you didn't stay here with us,
at night descended into the cellar instead
and didn't come back up again.
I am staggering, thoughts blurring,
time ran through our fingers.
Maybe I also am half dead already,
the tips of my toes on the first step of the staircase,
on the way down, into the cellar,
into the grave, in which I gave you.

The moments when one expects it the least
are the moments that can carry it the least.

And I carry you since then, heavy in my chest. Have no desire to bury you, or ask you, why are you gone already. Why is there this mark on my heart, black and blue, I don't really know how to describe it to you. My life now less full, more dull, as if someone killed a colour that is now missing. I think God misdialed, when he called you. Still, you descended into that cellar, to pick up the phone and give your life away.

You will be missed by me everyday.

In the moments when you should have been here, my wedding and other dreams coming true and you will be missed in the moments forever strange, when the sunrise washes up my grief for you.

You will be missed by me, in the moments that can carry it the least.
In the moments when I am still expecting you.

CLARA ZOELLNER
Green Concrete

Today I feel as if I'm not really here.
I've been left behind.

On the road. On the camping ground behind Bodmin Moor.
And I'm stuck in this green hiding the country lanes
I'm trying to find to get back home.

Yet, I am in my bed. Green sheets.
Lights breaking through the curtains
like trees on a summer afternoon
but the street is covered in fog
and the great British summer is just that,
Great British. With lots of rain and mud.

And I think about the winter months that I've endured with our high street flooding, whilst I stayed in bed, ill and tired from this rain and the cold. Our heating only on for 2 hours in the morning, working from home with a hot water bottle, and two blankets tucked around me.

Then, I dreamed of the great British summer.

Sunny in Cornwall, beach days and freshly cut watermelon with its juice running through my fingers. Hot sand between my toes and a sunburn on my nose.

Instead I am stuck.

On a field that I have already left, my brain already in the future far away, yet still mourning the summer that never came and the things I had to leave behind to be somewhat happy.

I will drive down the country lanes, for one last time to find myself in the muddy green fields and flee until my feet find the solid ground of the concrete freedom, never knowing if I will be all the better for it.

Yesterday I felt like I was not really here.
Today I've left it all behind.

CLARA ZOELLNER
Tainted

I am tired of the Saturday mornings
Still tasting like the Friday nights
Coffee and orange juice tainted by cider
and a bitter bile note threatens to come up
Boiling up to the surface alongside my fears
and reckless dreams seemingly shattered
on a dance floor littered by plastic cups
Too tender to break yet still destroyed

A floor too sticky to slip on, yet it feels like
I'm falling anyway, over into the wrong arms
or into the corner of the room where you stand
seemingly judging me, flailing arms, failing to arm myself
against your gaze, you unfazed, stoic face, widening space.

I start sinking into the wooden floor boards, that once held our love
like concrete in which I didn't see the cracks that I search for now to
swallow me up, so I don't have to look into your eyes and say

I miss you

Saturday mornings no longer taste like Friday nights and I lie to myself
that it's better this way. Boredom suits my wounded heart and I will
continue to taste the Saturday air in the Friday breeze until my heart
heals.

And yet, I still miss you

So sometimes I venture out into the dark
Imagine your figure passing through the park
Approach the bar that was our favourite spot
Try to keep distance, avoid getting caught
Yet ask your friends about your location
An addict with an unhealthy fixation
I don't know what to do to rid this feeling

My own thoughts rapidly unappealing
I don't want to miss you, I don't want to love you,
I just want to fall into someone else's arms and be
finally fucking fine with that

Saturday mornings taste like Saturday mornings
Life moves on so quickly, and I, no longer, miss you.

CONTRIBUTORS

Sebastian Adams
Would I recognise me, passing in the street, connect with myself in a group conversation? I wonder, would I regularly call? Would I get the feels when I spoke, smiling at every perfect imperfection? Would I enjoy the same pastimes when viewed from afar, laugh at every incredibly bad joke, get excited at how beautiful the world can be, watch sci-fi films, discuss their meaning, dance to electro swing, sing at the top of my voice to pop punk, get emotional at a beautifully written song? I wonder, would I fall in…(a parallel reflection)

Rhys Apollo
Here's my funky biography. I made it rhyme so it's fun to read: born up north, I fled down south, to grow and heal by flapping my mouth. I had a wonky start to life - lots of misery, pain and strife. I capture it now upon the page, furiously scribbling out my rage. I sing of my past shameful antics and explore my minds tocks and ticks. I'll ramble on about any subject, picking a topic to dissect and inspect. God, grief, tinder, cheese. I write to heal, I write to please.

Archie
My name is Archie/Ash De Haldevang, I am a Third Year Film student, doing my best and writing poems. I have been doing it for a long time and am still enjoying it.

Frances Bennett
I am a fiddle player and teacher and have enjoyed creative writing for many years, often inspired by life in my native Cornwall and particularly by its folk music and language. An obsessive reader and diary writer, I've lived in France, Spain and Switzerland and these experiences also tend to crop up in my work.

Alex Blaby
Alex Blaby is motivated to write by alternative travel and adventures. One particular piece of surreal fiction was inspired by a two week experience in which he was the warden of an island off the coast of

Cornwall. During his time there, he developed characters to occupy the many benches which were ideally situated at various viewpoints.

Zak Bowden
My name is Zak. I'm a student of Evolutionary Biology, and I've been writing poetry for about 12 months. I started writing during a dark time in my life and found it really allowed me to inject some levity into life and to laugh at the absurdity of it all. Moth Tales was the first place I've ever read anything I'd written and I've never had anything but a lovely time there.

Lesley Chandler
The poem 'Polly's Pancake Pantoum' and other pieces were a by-product of lockdowns during the Covid epidemic. A friend invited me to join her online creative writing group for wellbeing. This was the result of playing around with favourite foods from childhood. I'm still in the group, still writing and still feeling
(fairly) well!

India Childs
India Childs is a Poet and Writer living in Falmouth Cornwall and has been performing some of her work at Open Mics since she was a teenager. A lot of her work is centred on observations, inspired by real people that she encounters either only briefly, or more formative influences from her own friends and experiences. India has attended MothTales since the very first Open Mic!

James Croftson
James started writing songs at school, after learning a few chord shapes on an old hand-me-down guitar. Although free-time for writing and playing seems to be in ever-shorter supply, the enthusiasm is still there, when the busyness of life allows. These days, the opportunity for any of this is usually limited to mentally writing lyrics whilst cycling to and from work; the ability to multi-task well enough to play guitar whilst doing this is something not yet mastered. This has led to him pondering the distinction between 'songs without music', and 'poetry': where does one end and the other begin; is there really a distinction at all? James

lives with his wife and children near Falmouth, and works in the offshore renewables industry.

Kim Croftson
"Let's pretend I'm a pianist, playing all day long; practising tirelessly, breaking ground in song. Let's pretend I'm a writer filling up the page: words to define anything, assuage or enrage. Let's pretend I'm a daughter, eating up the years; working for the family, catching all the tears. Let's pretend I'm a mother, righting all the wrongs; upholding principles. Let's pretend I'm strong. Let's pretend I'm strong". Quartogenerian Kim Croftson lives in a cosy house near Falmouth with her young family, and her imaginary Old English Sheep dog….. perhaps one day that gorgeous animal will become a real dog!

Alan Cummings
Alan Cummings has been alive for more than seven decades. He has been a gymnast, a scientist, a picture restorer, a lover, a husband, a father, a songwriter, a performer, a scuba diver, a Professor and a Pro Vice Chancellor. He is currently President of the Royal Cornwall Polytechnic Society (the Poly) in Falmouth. Mostly, he likes finding words that seem as if they belong together and mean something to himself or someone else.

Mike Dempsey
I'm Mike. I've been married for nearly 30 years to Carol. We have grown up children and grandchildren. I work as a Theatres Recovery Nurse which means I wake people up after operations. I started writing poetry after hearing a great best man poem at a wedding. Then when I was a best man I did the same and it went down a storm. I started writing for birthday parties etc. Then wrote more personal (not so funny) stuff and took them to Open Mics and Folk Nights. I love the flow of poems and songs. I love to hear what I once heard described as " a man of quiet poetry" – someone who uses unusual words and phrases in everyday speech like Cornish farmers or people I've known due to my Irish roots. They don't even know they're poets!

Mac Dunlop
Mac is a poet, composer and performer based in Cornwall, UK. He

recently published 26 Voices for Change, an anthology of 26 Cornish writers published by the Poetry Point Press. Other publications include: Solarium - written while Poet in Residence with the National Trust - and The Enigma Deviations. Recent digital audio releases include A Song for Carla Bley, Viral Nature, and Somewhere Nearby. His work features on BBC Sounds, Resonance FM and other mainstream broadcasters.

Chloé Eathorne
Chloé Eathorne is a Cornish Poet and visual artist interested in exploring the underbelly of Cornwall through her writing, the rust and pride that lies beneath the glossy sheen of tourist paraphernalia. She hosts The Wildflower Hour, discussing art, poetry & mental health on Source FM.

Vincent Gould
Vincent Gould is a performance poet, musician and actor. He has been making songs, poems, satire and video for the last two decades. He has performed at Edinburgh Festival and on BBC TV and radio. He is based in Birmingham.

Lauren Gauge
Lauren Gauge is an award-winning pansexual writer, performer, director and producer of poetry and plays. She writes both for stage and screen about and with women, mothers, queer and working-class communities - celebrating stories of where she grew up that empower people, connection, and create transformative art for everyone, regardless of background or place. Her work has appeared in London's West End, Bristol Old Vic, and the Palace theatres of Belarus. Her debut poem-turned-gig-theatre-play, The Unmarried, won the Hive & Lyric Hammersmith New Writing Award, premiered at Lyric Hammersmith and was later selected as Pick of the Fringe in Underbelly, Edinburgh after a sell-out run of UK festivals. Lauren is one of four commissioned writers on attachment to The Minack Theatre on their Emerging Playwright Programme 2023. Lauren is currently developing a TV version of The Unmarried supported by Off West End Plays and Playwrights.

Paul Hackett
I have lived in Cornwall for three and a half years. Two years ago I went to a folk night, and found to my surprise the ability to write the spoken word.

Darshan Harode
Darshan is a wildlife and underwater photographer and filmmaker currently studying second year at Falmouth University. He likes to explore the natural world and going on a walk. His music interest is quite diverse and he likes to hear other's stories.

Maisy Inston
Maisy Inston doesn't so much write poems as wait until they hit her, often on trains or, perhaps more annoyingly, as she's just falling asleep. Central to all things in her life is her love of animals (primarily bats) and the natural world, and she spends all her time researching, drawing, writing and singing about it. She lives in Falmouth but has a long distance relationship with her cat, Mali (also known as 'The Marl') whom she also writes about.

Jeremy Johnson
I have been called from beyond, but returned. Father, MacGyver chef, masochistic bassist, sometime songwriter, reluctant poet.

Peter King
Pete King lives on the Helford Estuary with his wife and their golden retriever. Before coming to Cornwall 9 years ago he taught in various universities and wrote 3 books on the history of crime and justice in England c.1700-1870. Before that he had 4 years as a social worker. He also trained as a Christian minister which was not especially successful but did lead to his current role as a chaplain at Falmouth/Exeter University. He combines this with supporting his wife who is building a contemplative garden behind their house.

Siddharth Unnithan Kumar
Siddharth studied mathematics at the University of Oxford, where he recently completed a PhD with a thesis at the intersection of geography, mathematics, ecology and anthropology, titled 'Mathematical

ecology in a more-than-human world'. Siddharth is now doing a postdoctorate with the University of Exeter, exploring the relationships between humans and the natural world, and between inner and outer worlds of human experience. He can be contacted at: siddharth.unnithankumar@gmail.com.

Matt McCoy
I am a creative, culturally curious word slinger, equally intrigued by the mundane and the mysterious. A builder of bold, imaginary worlds to escape into as ours falls apart, I take solace that the greatest stories reside within all of us. I write facts and fiction and sometimes a mixture of both.

Seb Ramdin
Poetry has helped me positively express my feelings. To live healthily and not set fire to relationships I have with myself and others, I lean into emotional pain that can appear and nurture it. Writing and performing validate my version of the world and this will save my life. You should try it too; poetry is everybody's place to express themselves.

Andrew Searle
Since moving to Cornwall, I have been inspired to write poems that bring me closer to this beautiful place and its rich history. It's been an incredible start to a poetry journey that I hope will continue for years and it's been a pleasure to do this within such a wonderful community.

Alex Small
Alex Small is better known locally for his passions of classic cars and paddle boarding as his alter ego, Classicaraddict. He has been writing and performing since 2010 after enrolling with Falmouth University.

Phil Thomson
Phil Thomson MA FRSA is a writer and artist with many years experience as an educator in the world of Visual Communication. His early professional life was spent in the design and advertising industry as a creative director and copy writer, at the same time gaining a reputation as a widely published lyricist, with a range from hymns with Hodder & Stoughton to being recorded by Sir Cliff Richard. These

days, he is out and about with his novel, 'Momentary lapses in concentration' a book of his photography with poems by Gregory Leadbetter, and, of course, a book of his own poetry.

Frankie de Vos
Frankie is a young poet originally from Swindon, now a computer science student at Falmouth University.   He started writing poetry when he was 15 years old and since moving to Falmouth he has performed his own work at Moth Tales every month.

Grenville Watts
My name is Grenville and I'm a European coach driver who drives all over Europe. I travel to lots of fantastic places but nowhere truly beats Falmouth. Originally from the Black Country in the Midlands, but home is now Falmouth and my heart and love is now always in Falmouth. I write poetry and song lyrics on many different subjects, always trying to write from my heart and my soul. If just a few people are touched or moved by my words, then I always feel truly honoured

Clara Zoellner
Clara grew up as a third culture kid across Asia and Europe before finding a sense of home in Cornwall. Her writing reflects on the ongoing struggle between fighting and embracing her urge of constant transition with an aim to find meaning in the madness life can be.

ACKNOWLEDGEMENTS

Over the months, since the pilot event late in 2022, Moth Tales has been supported by a wonderful staff team. Thank you, Matt, Lindsey, Raz, Debby, Elli, Rhi, John, Caitlin, Lexi, Claire, Nicole, and Alex for creating the perfect character and atmosphere at The Moth & The Moon for our spoken word community to flourish.

Thank you also to Matt Johnson for the illustrations and cover design

Davaar
Heavens Might

For my shield this day, I call
Heavens might;
Suns Brightness
Moons Whiteness
Fires glory
Lightnings swiftness
Winds wildness
Oceans depth
Earth solidity
Rocks immobility
Each others enduring love

APS PUBLICATIONS